RETRO

Old Fashioned Christmas

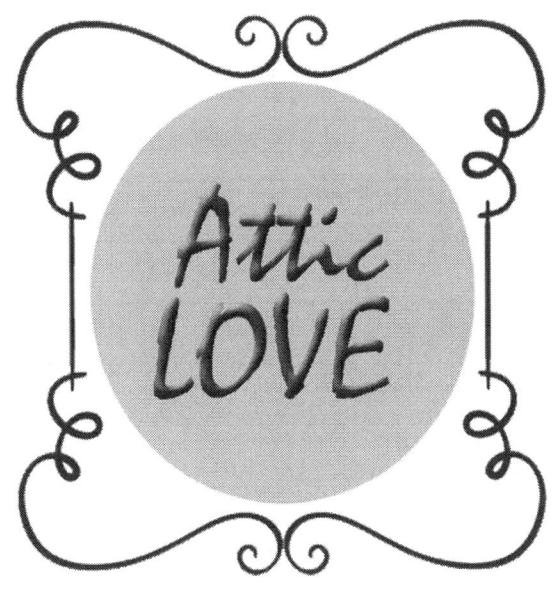

Why Coloring in Greyscale?

When coloring over greyscale try to think of it as a color by numbers for adults (Just without the numbers.)

The darkness or lightness of the grey will be your guide and will show you how dark or light color you should use and exactly where on the image you should use it.

Light colors over light grey areas, dark colors over dark grey areas, and the medium colors in between.

When coloring this way you will get the look of shading without having to shade at all - providing the depth which is so hard to achieve on a traditional coloring page.

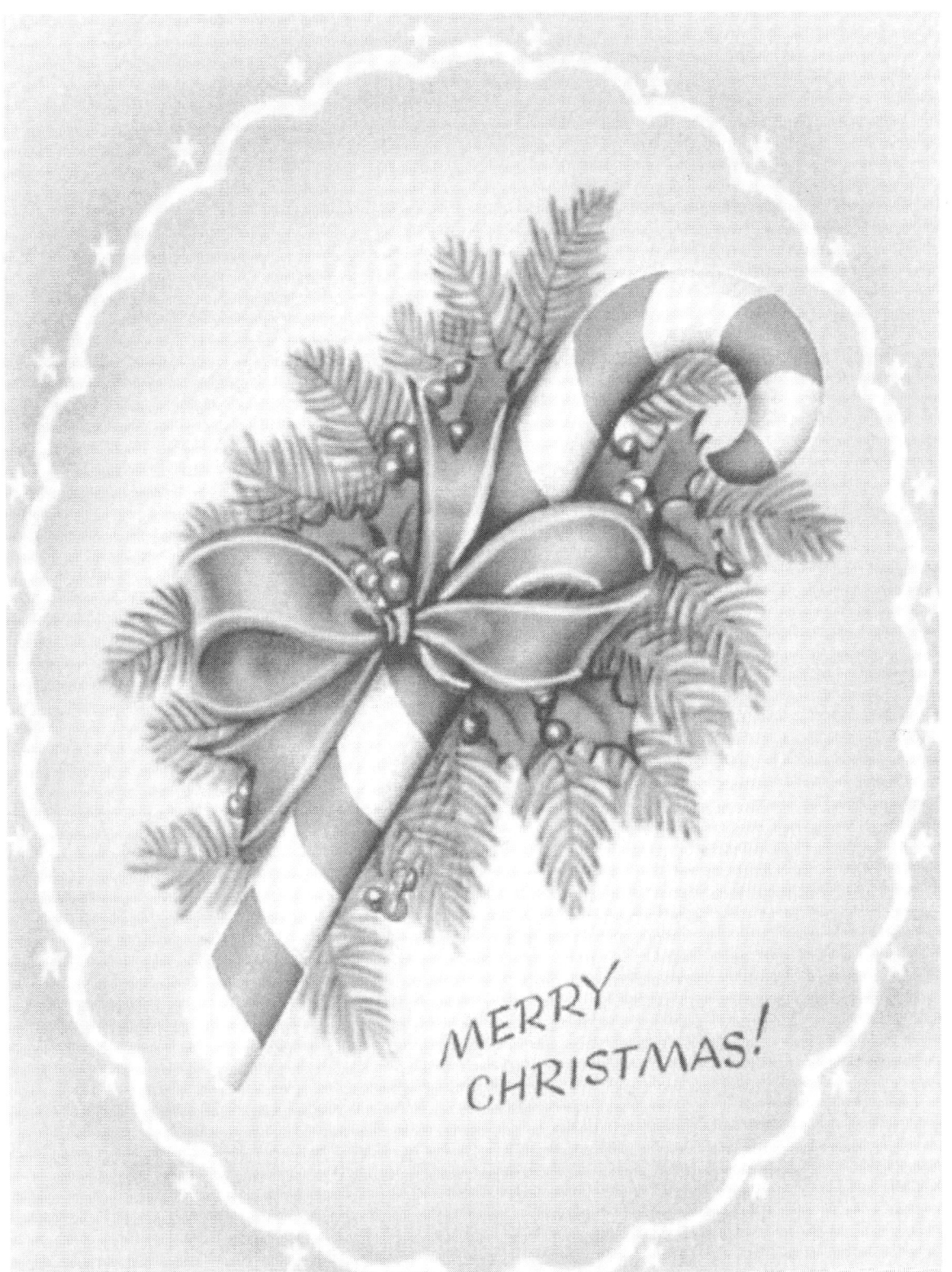

MERRY CHRISTMAS!

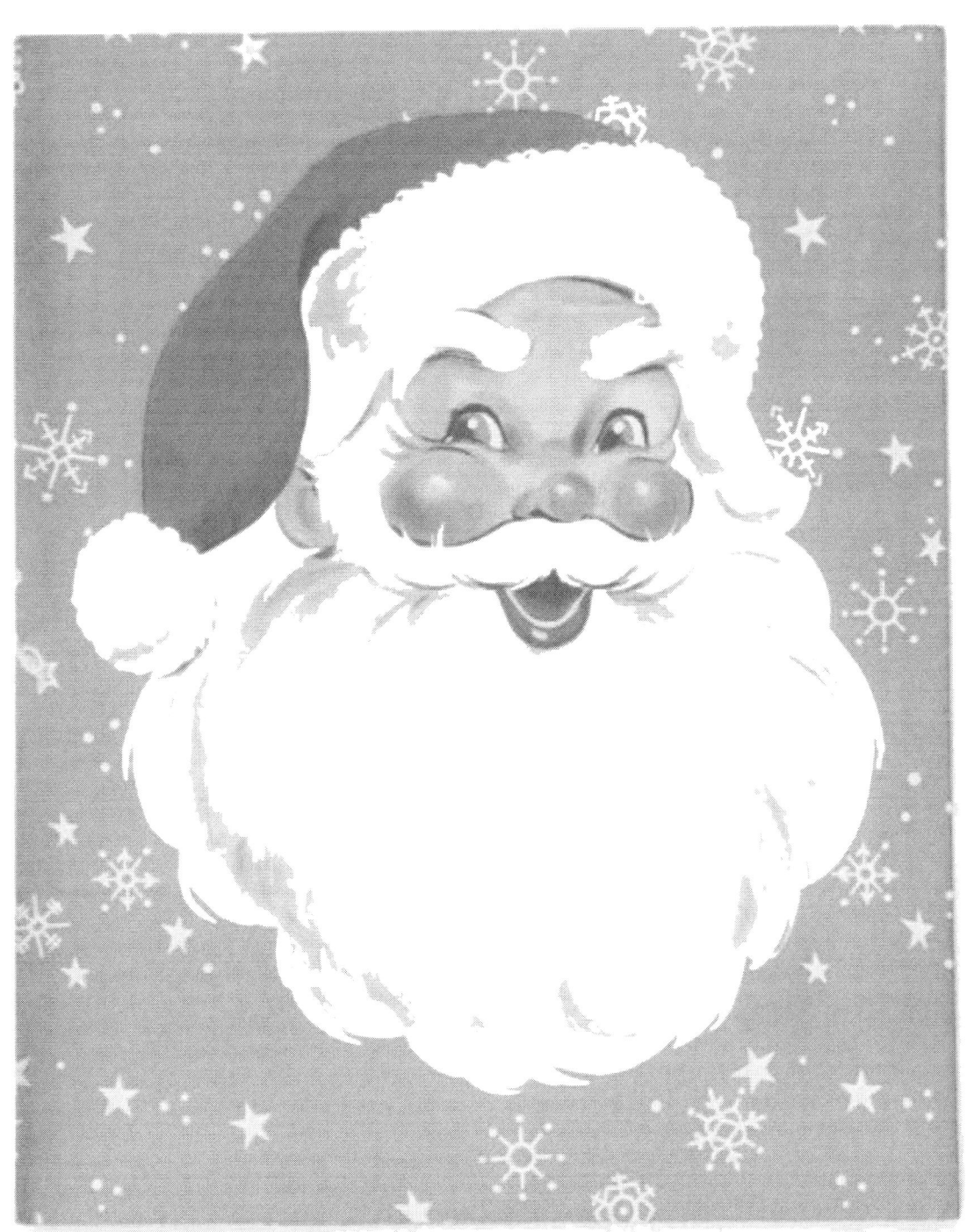

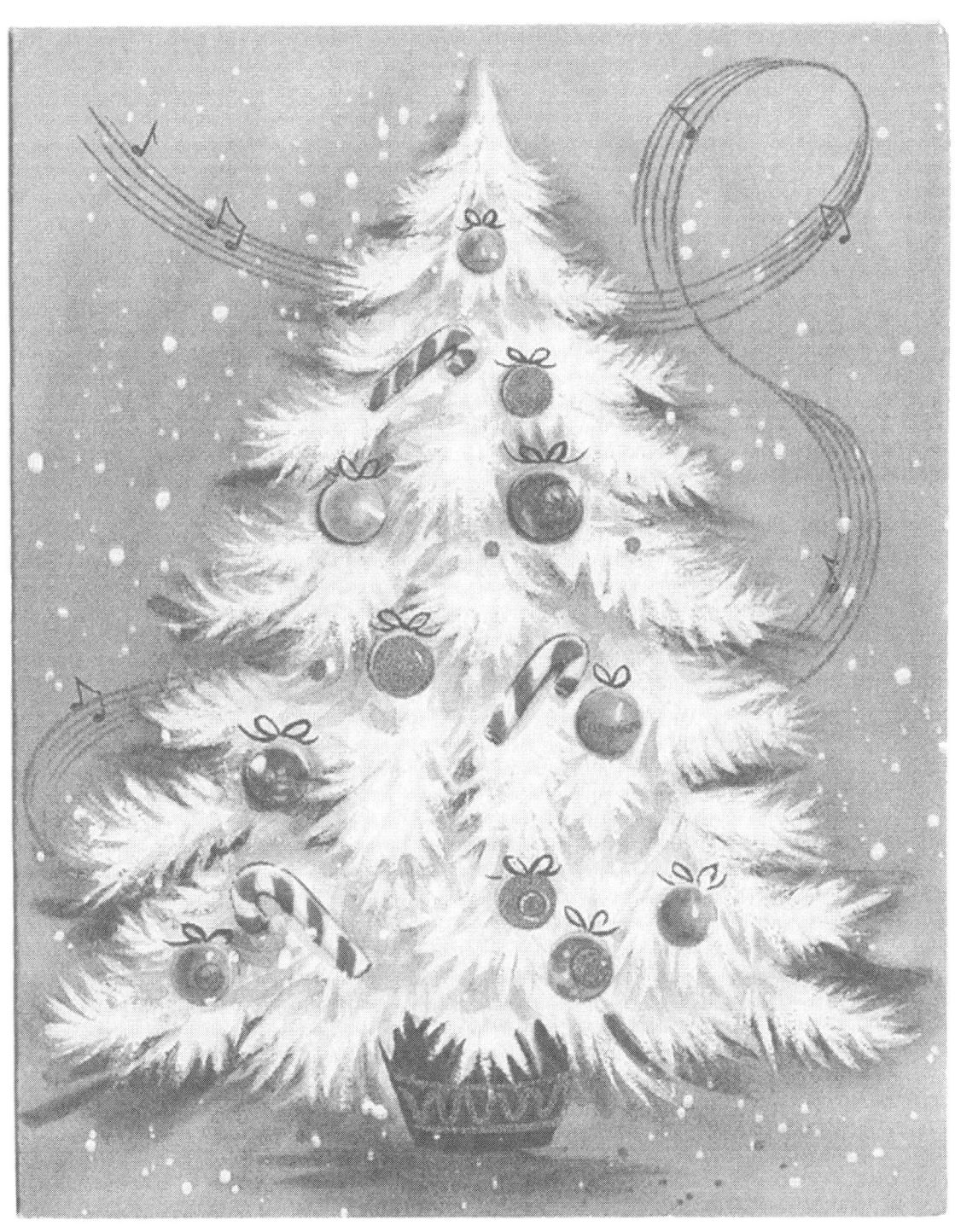

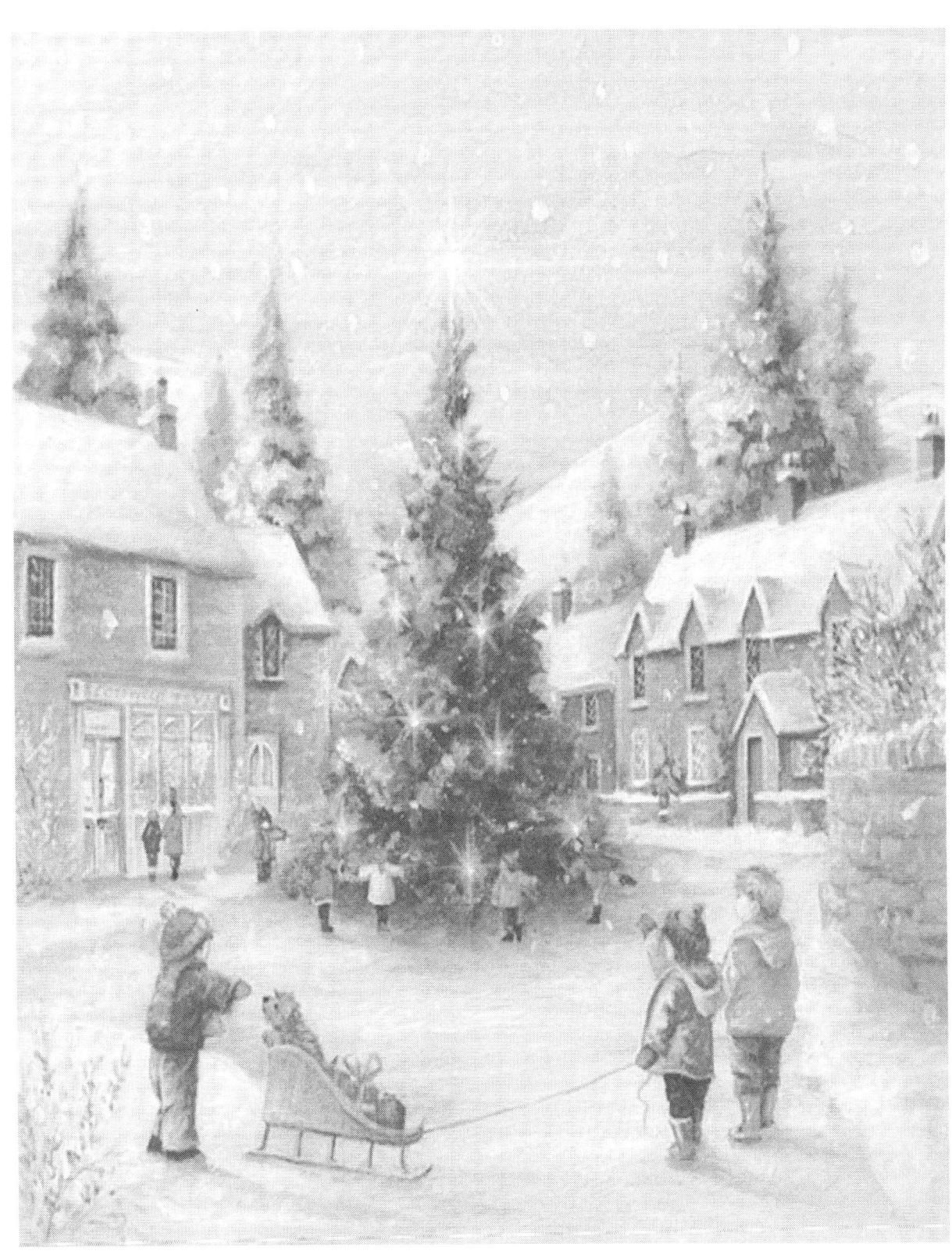

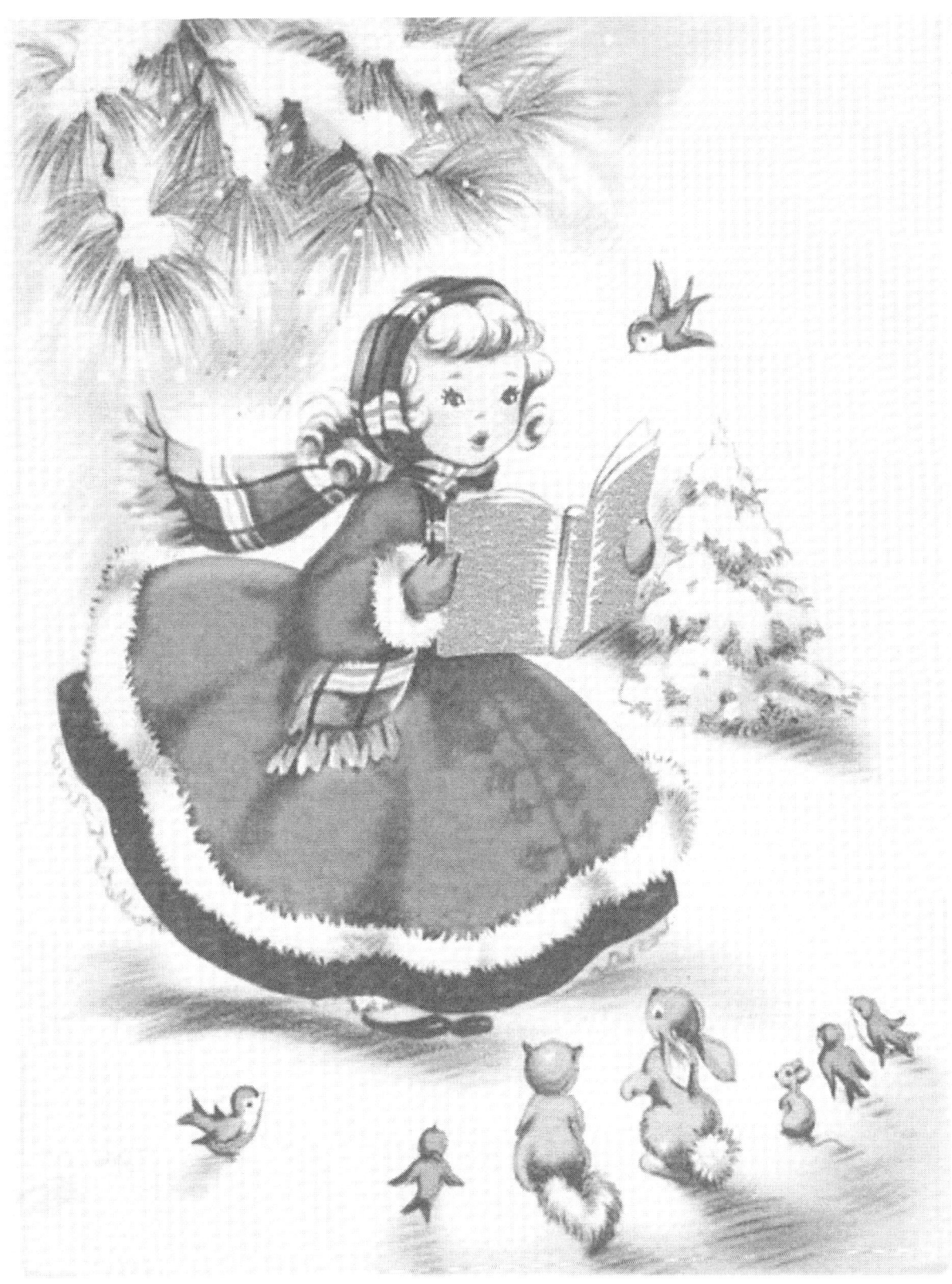

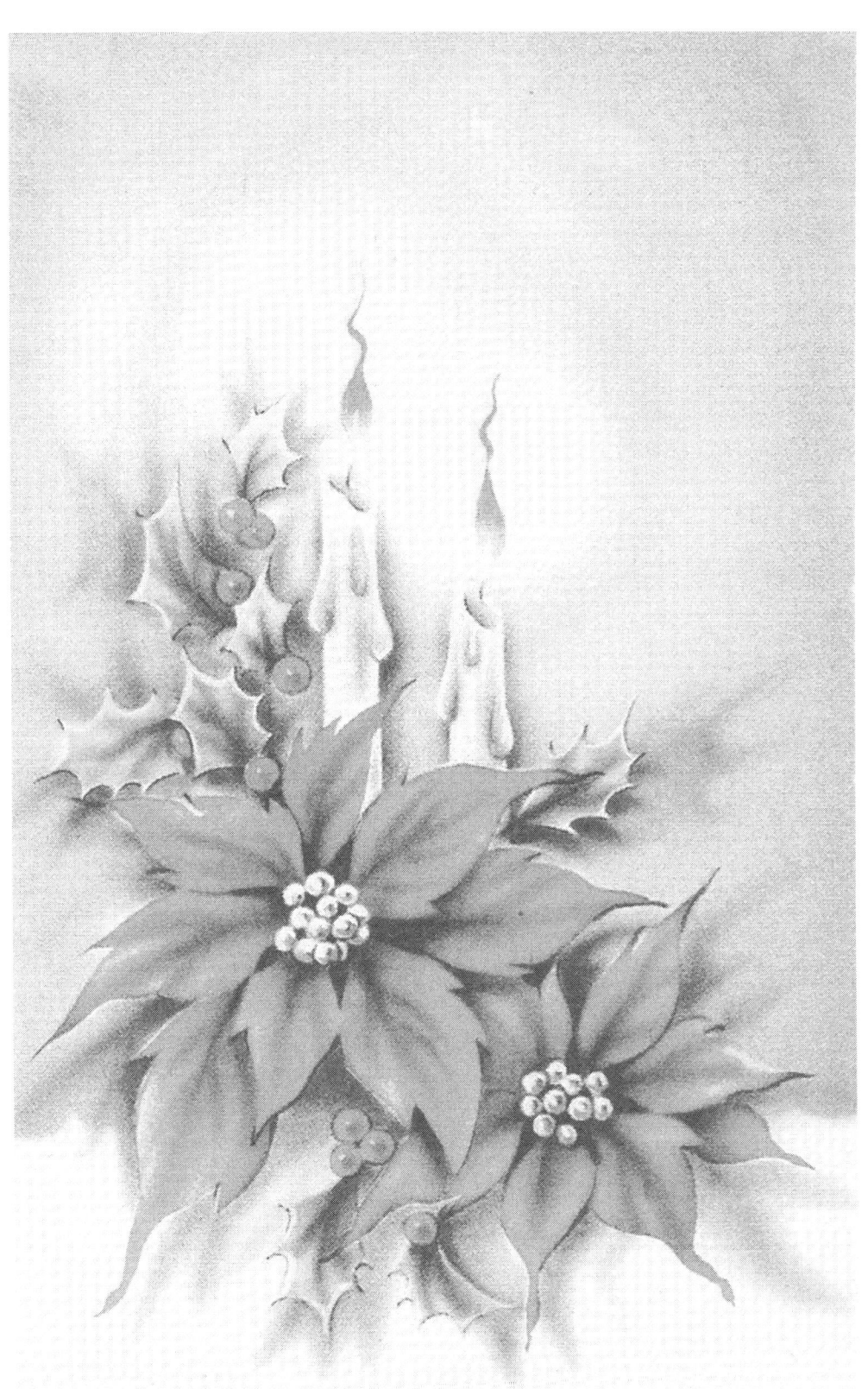

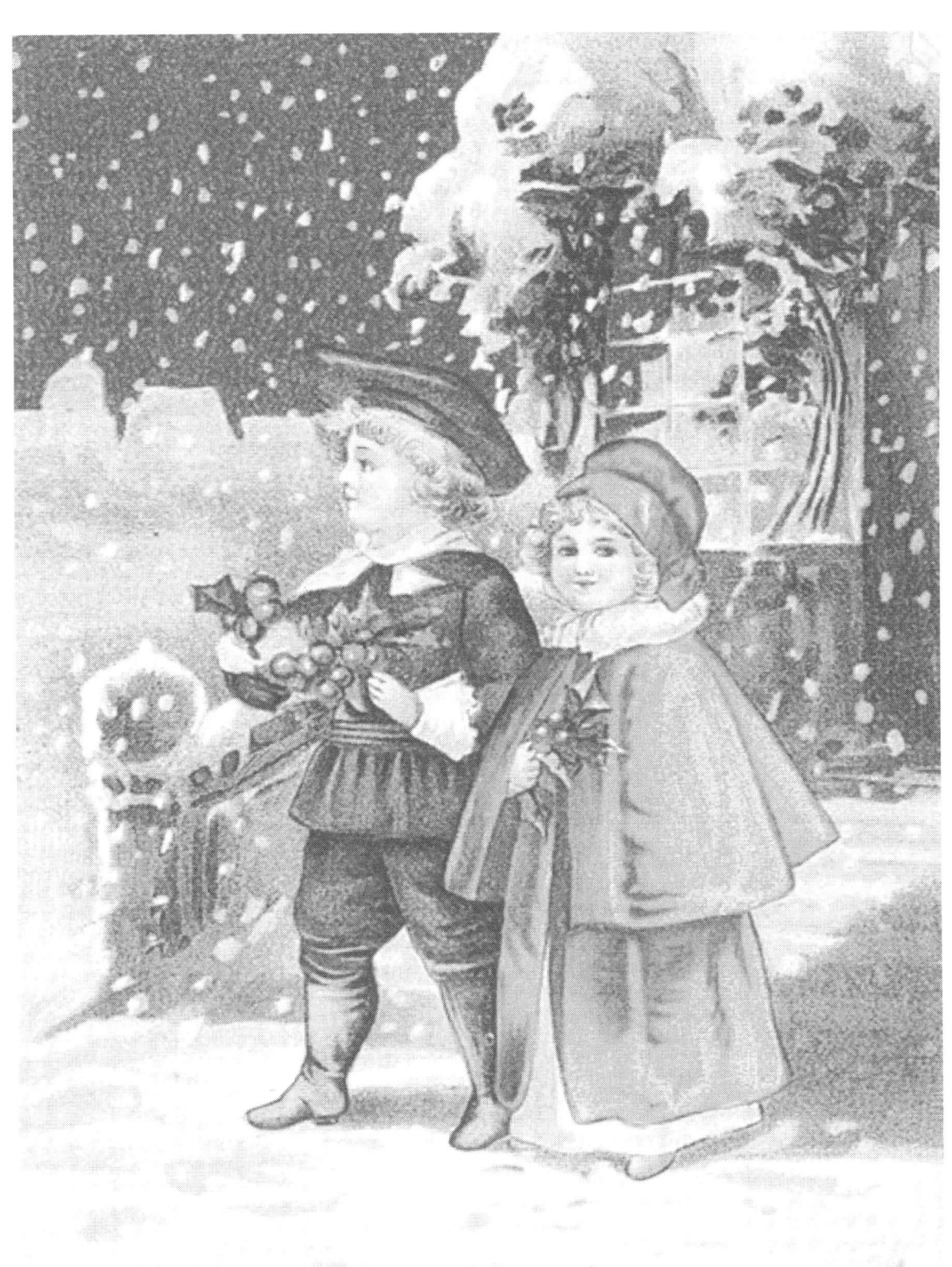

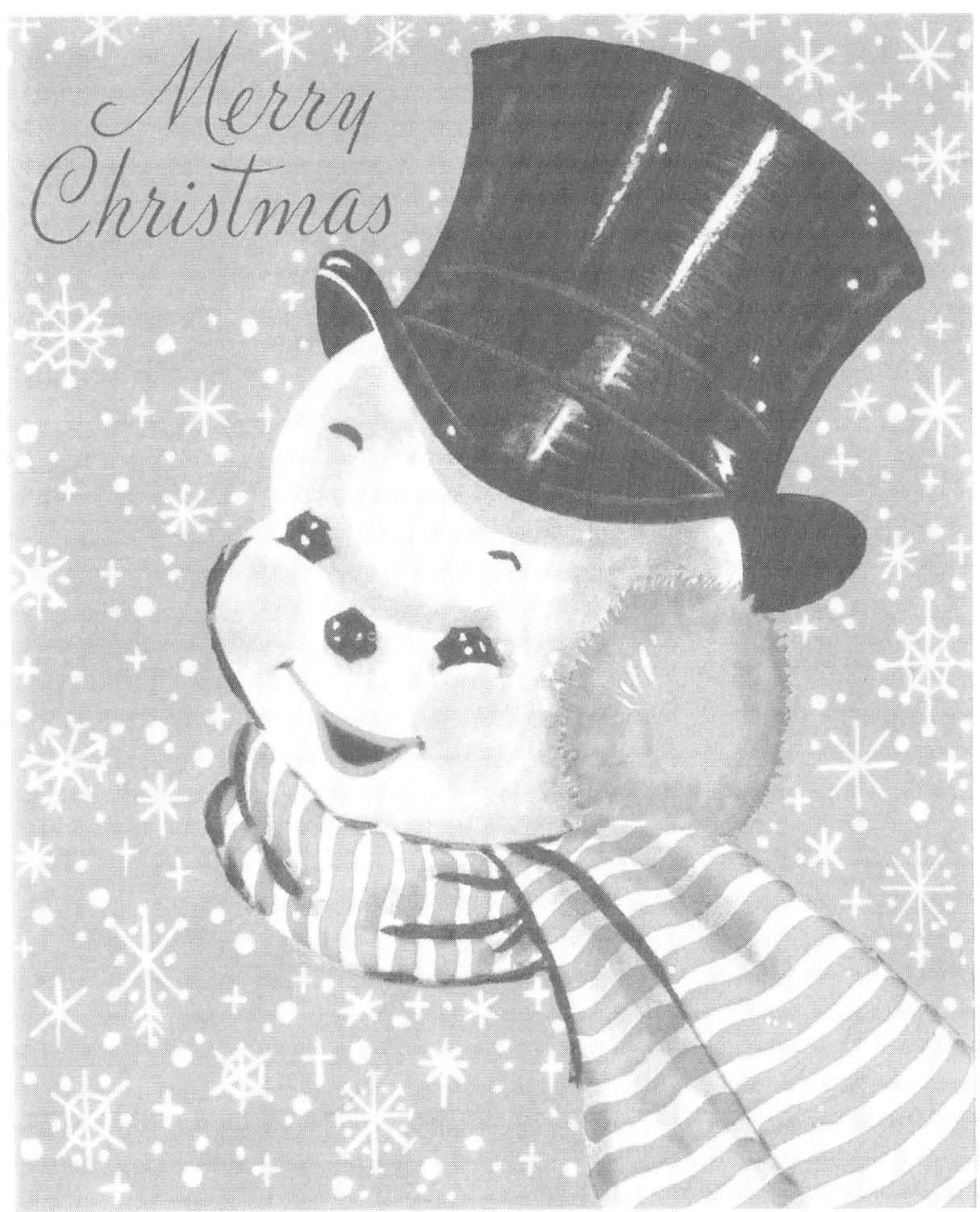

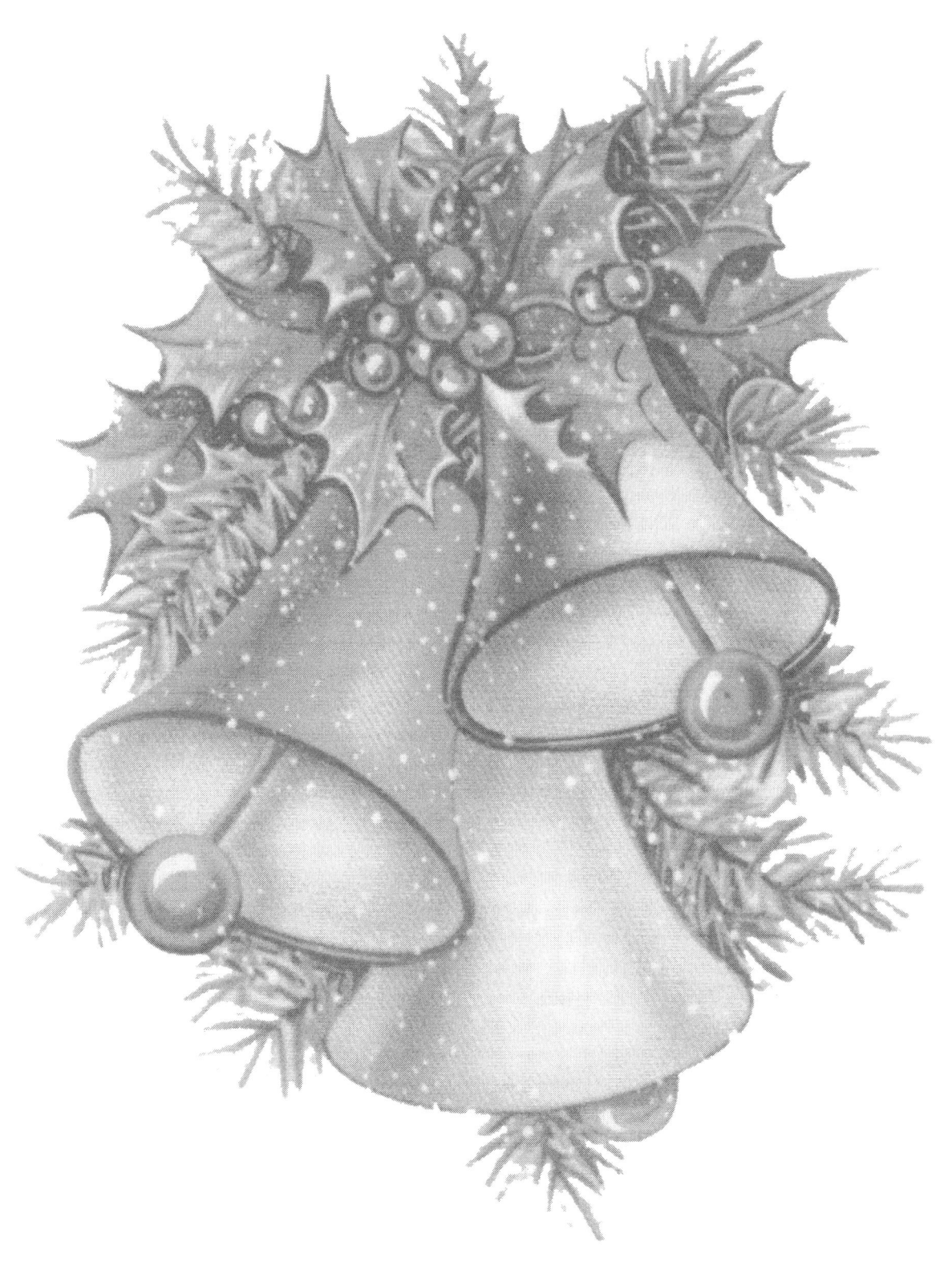

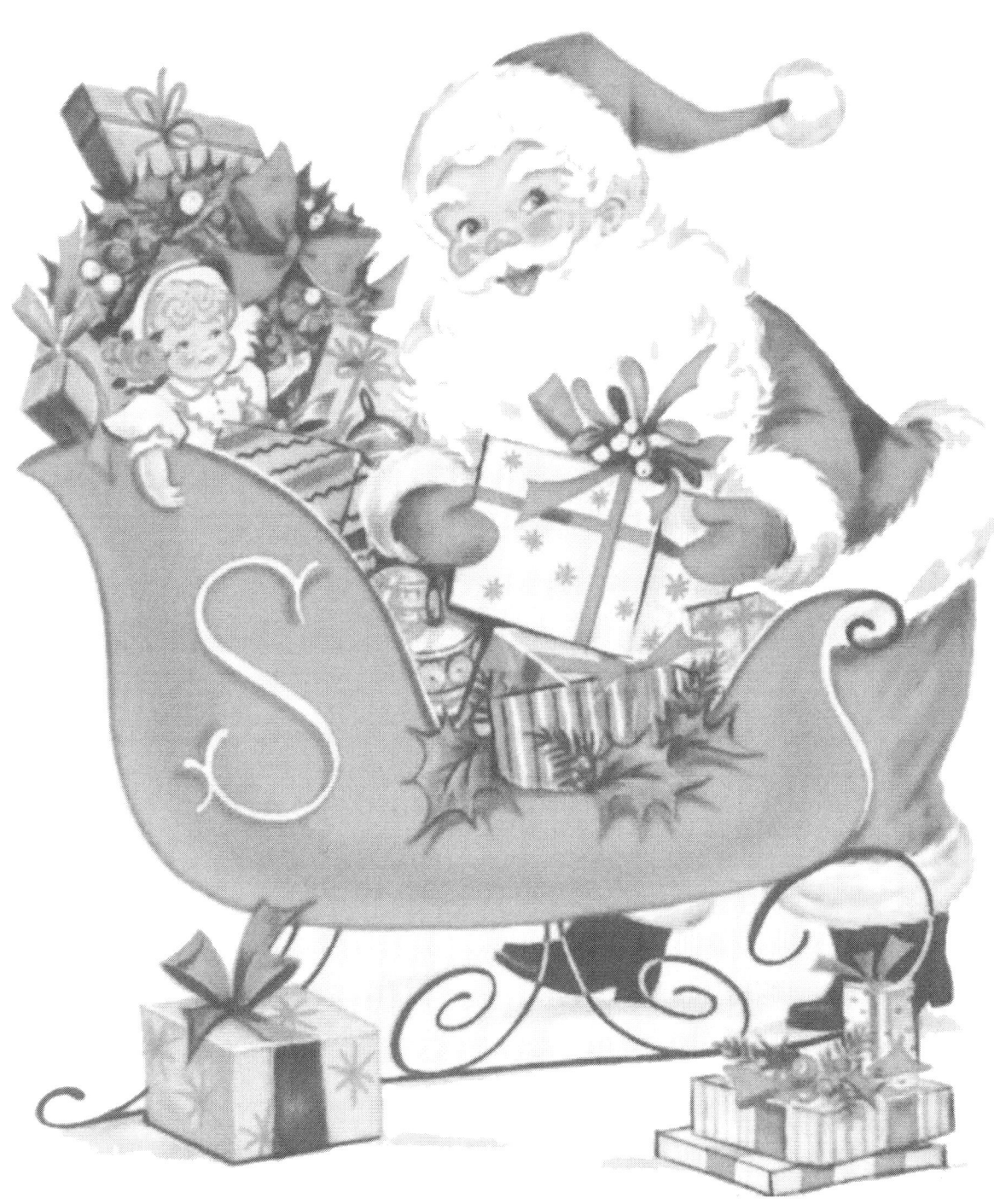

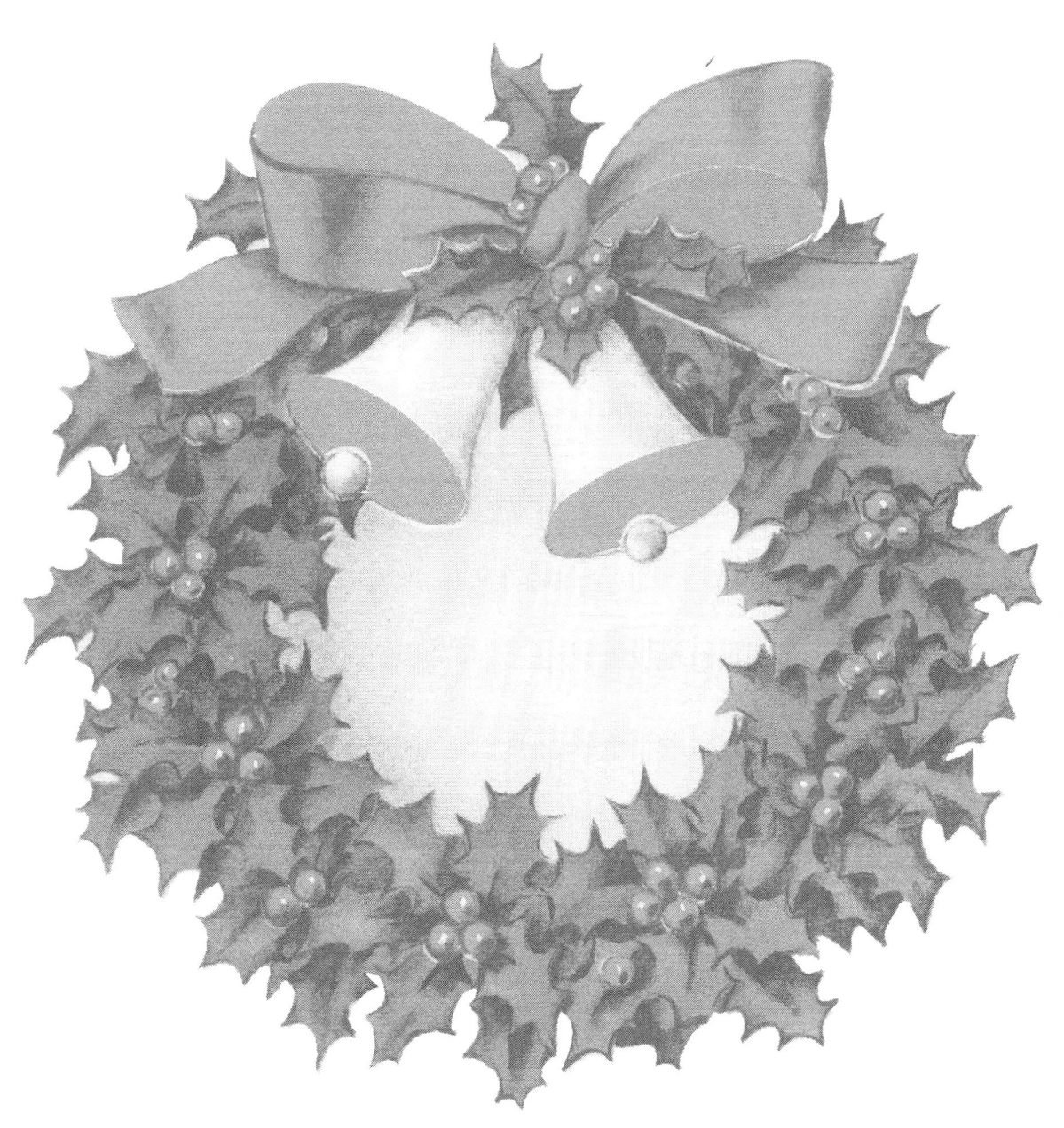

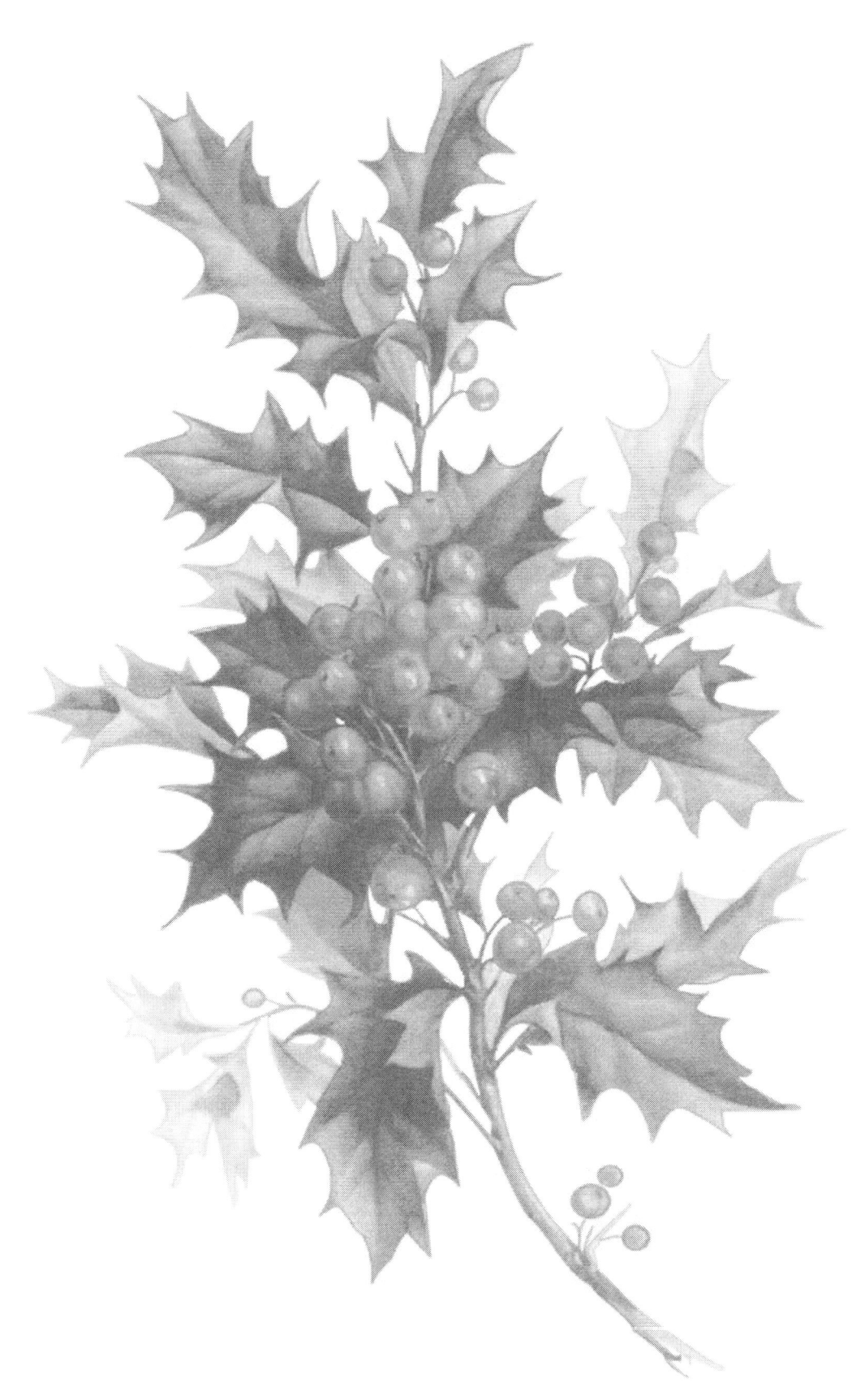

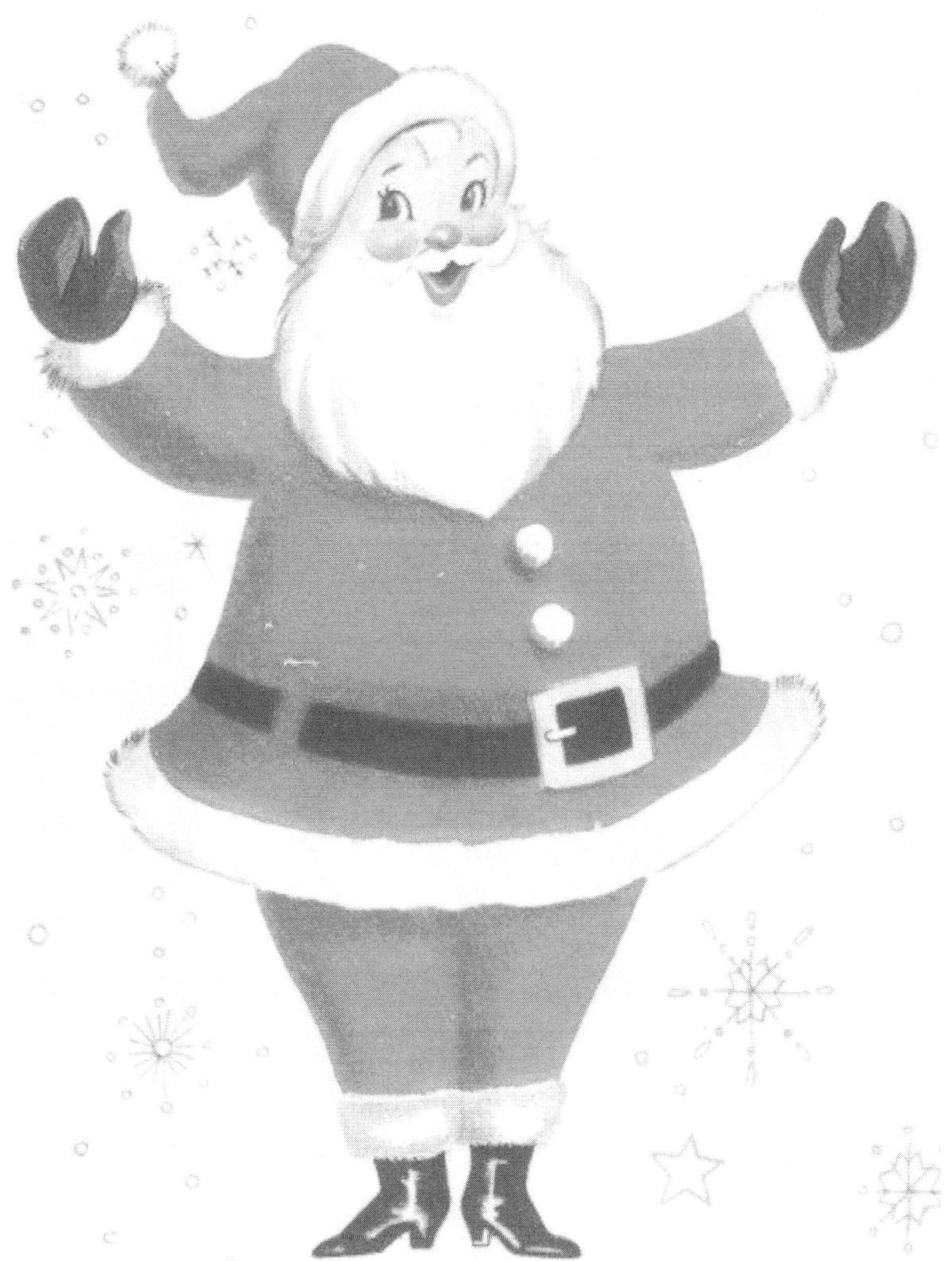

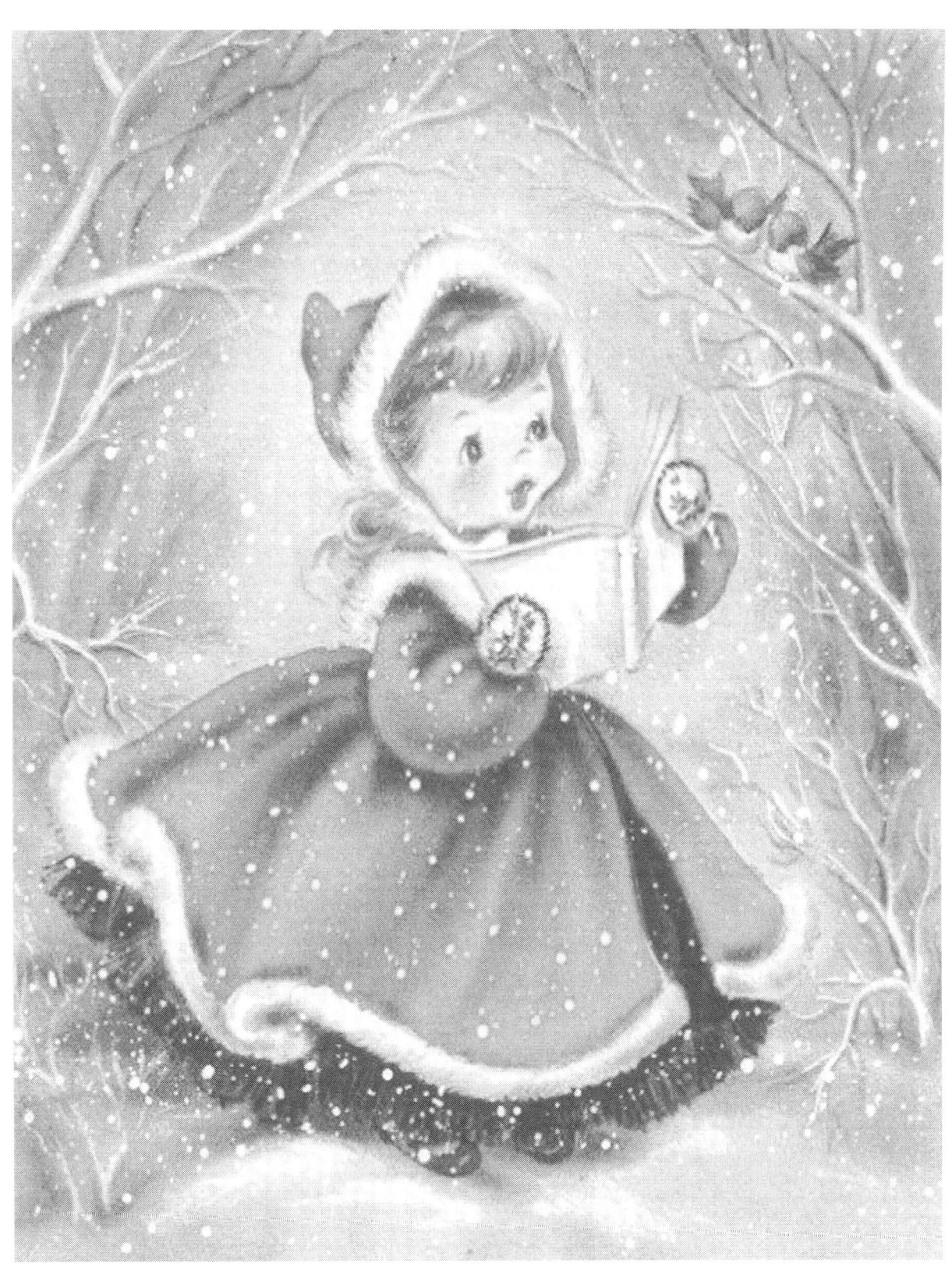

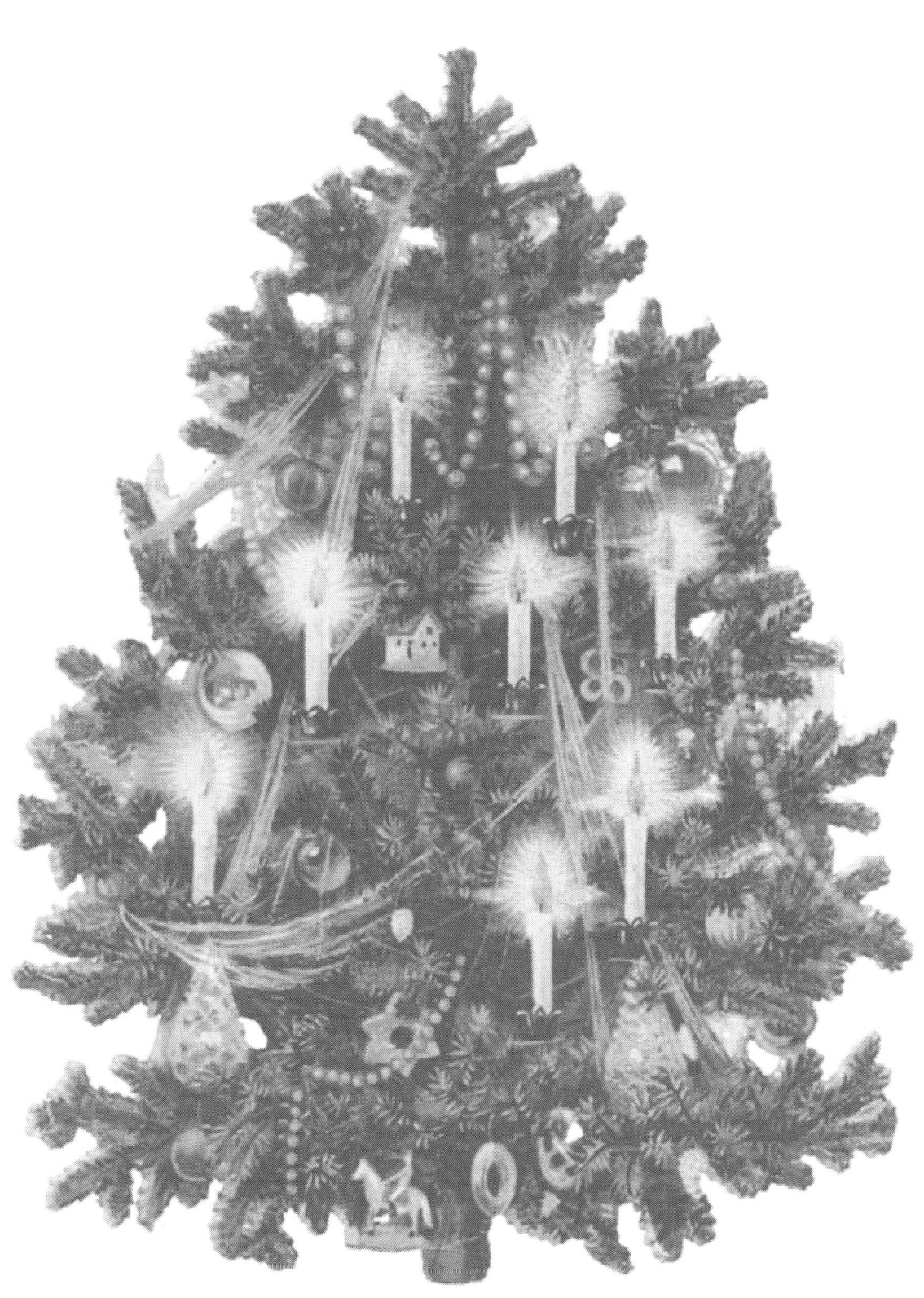

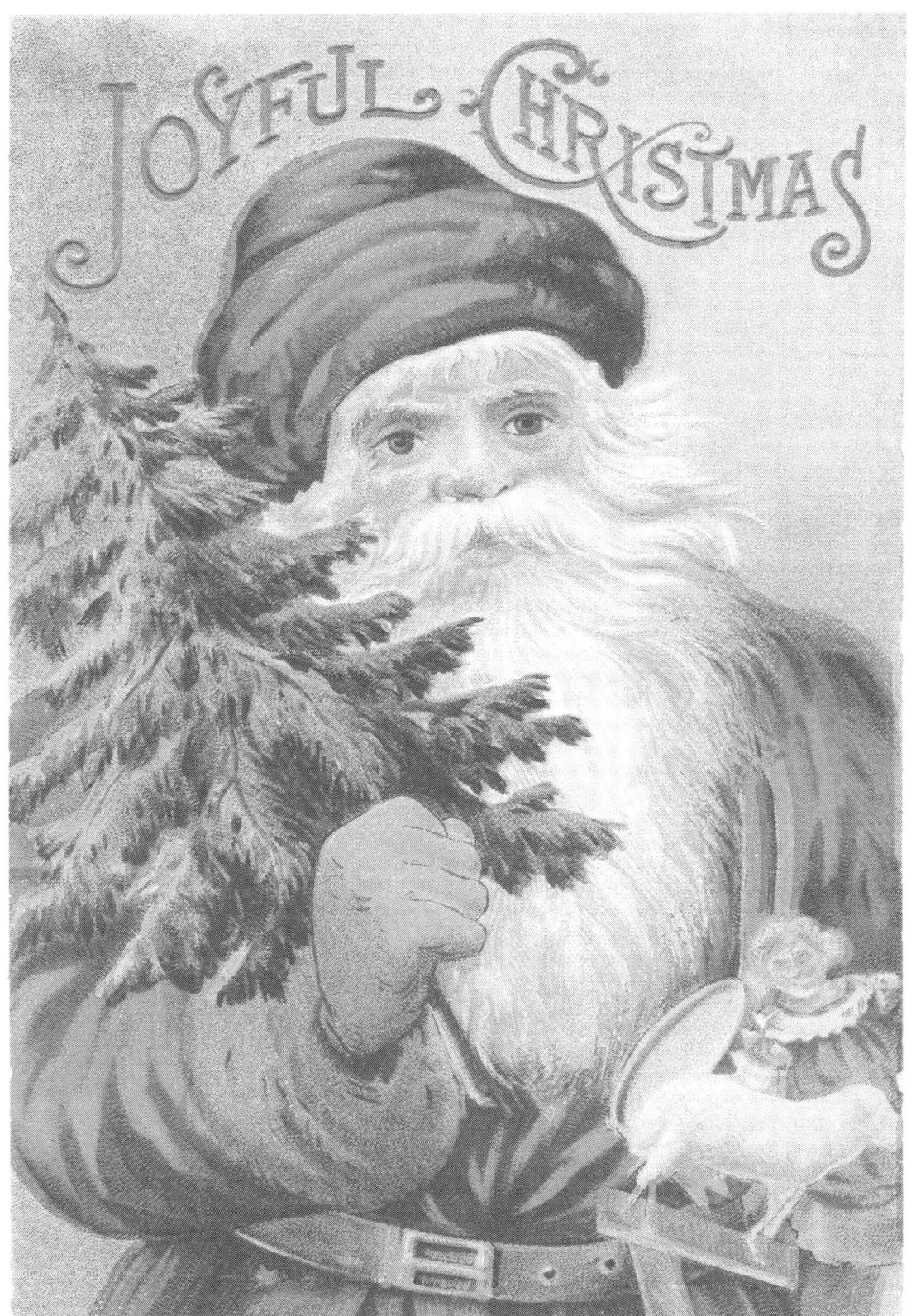

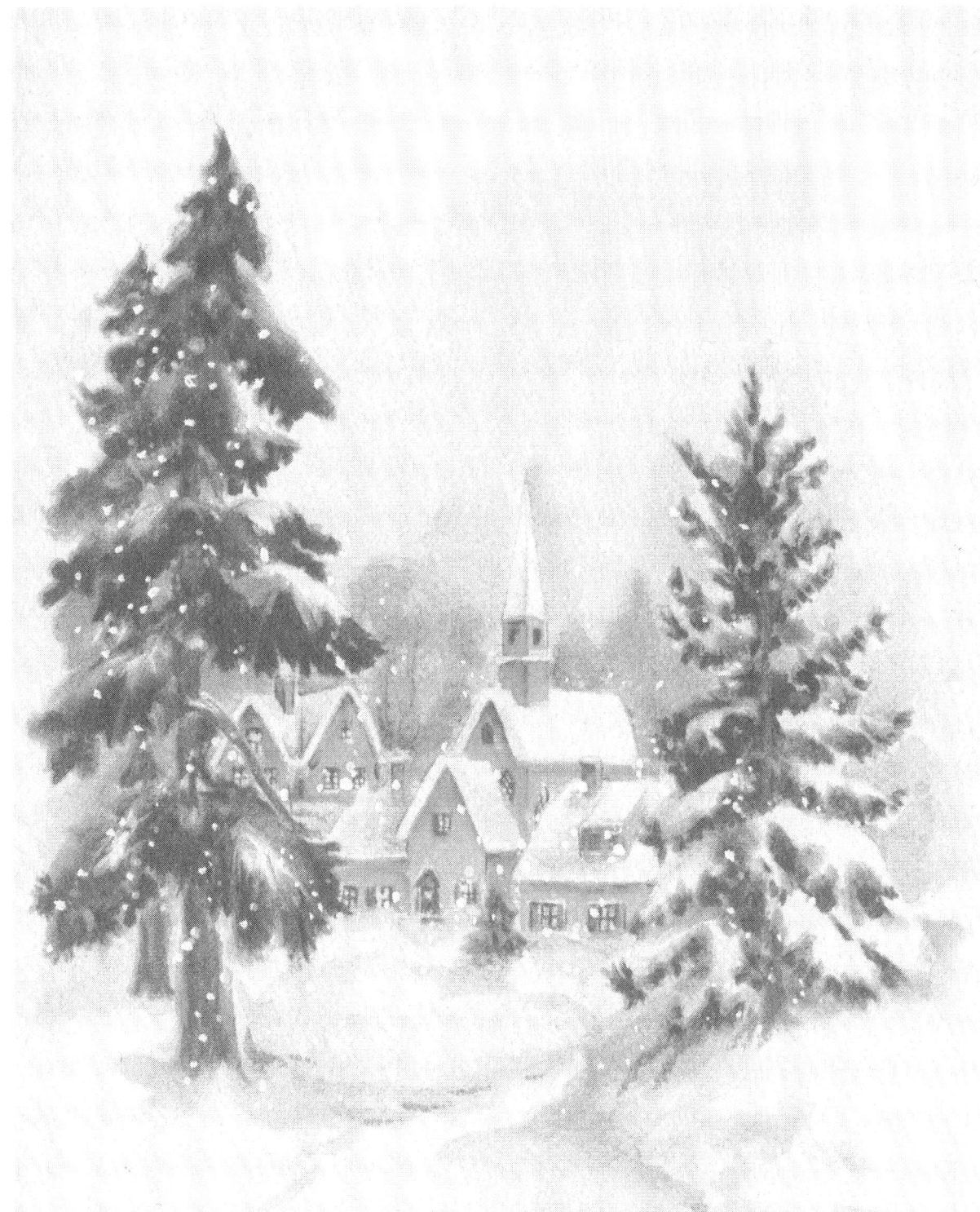

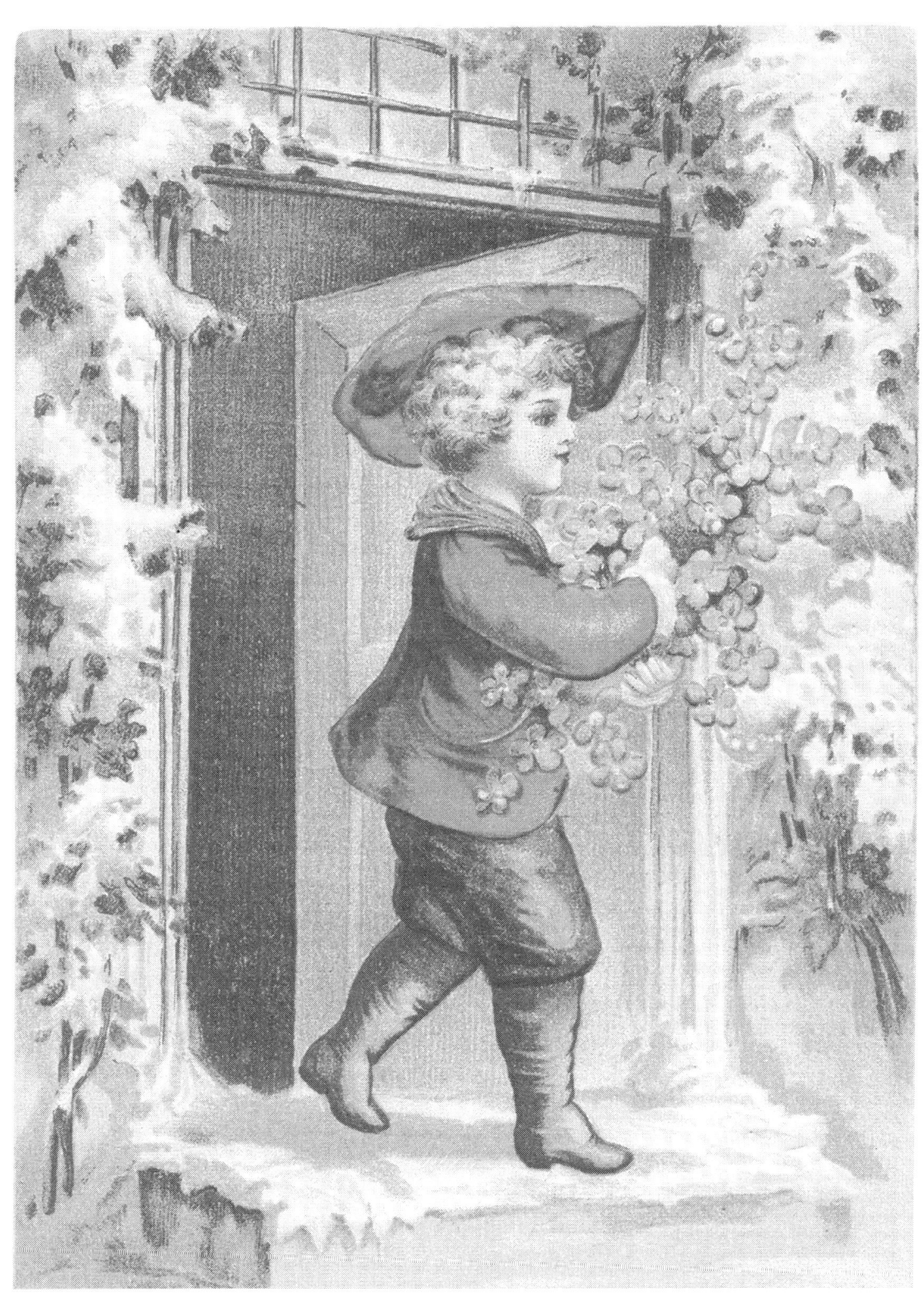

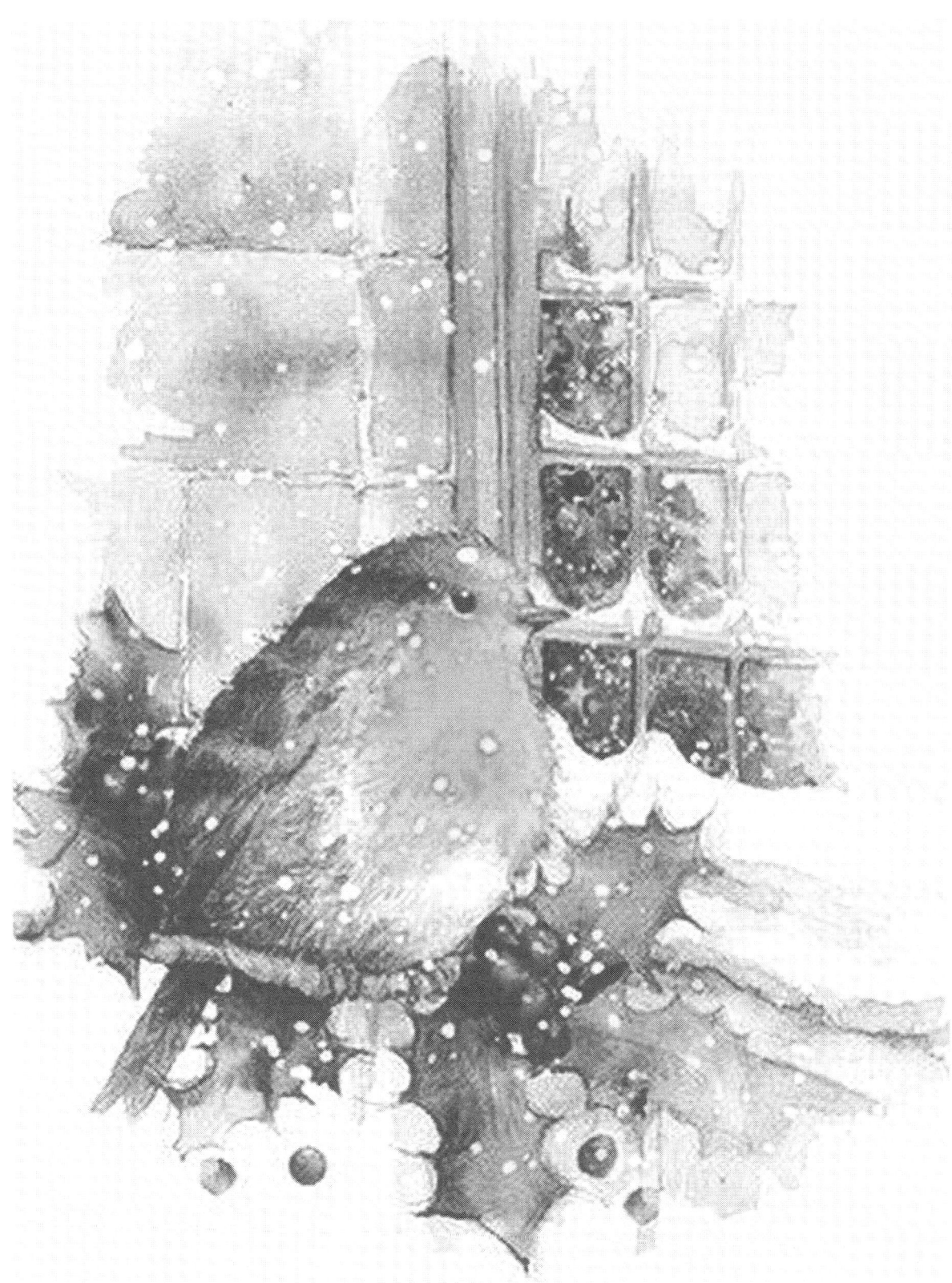

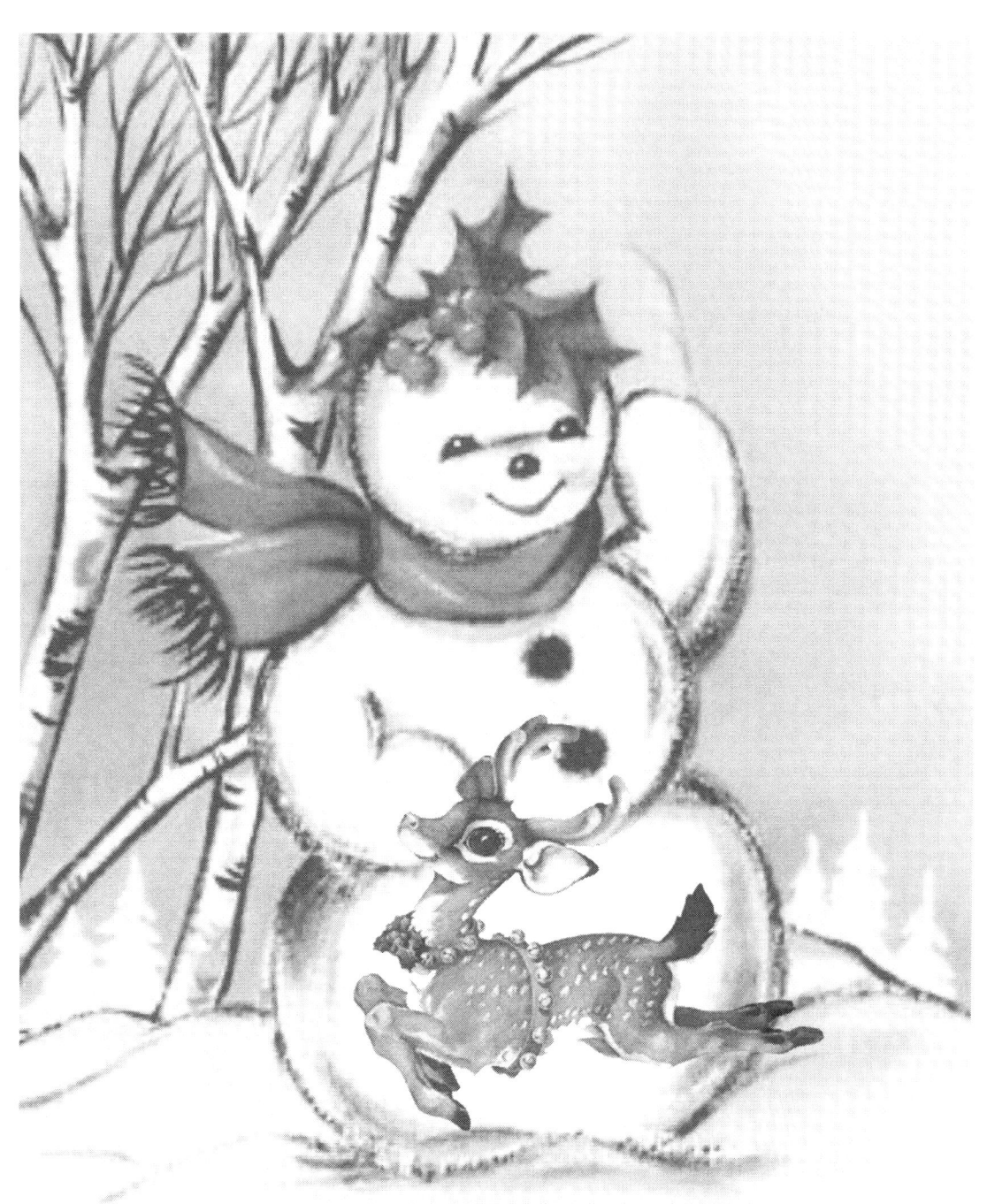

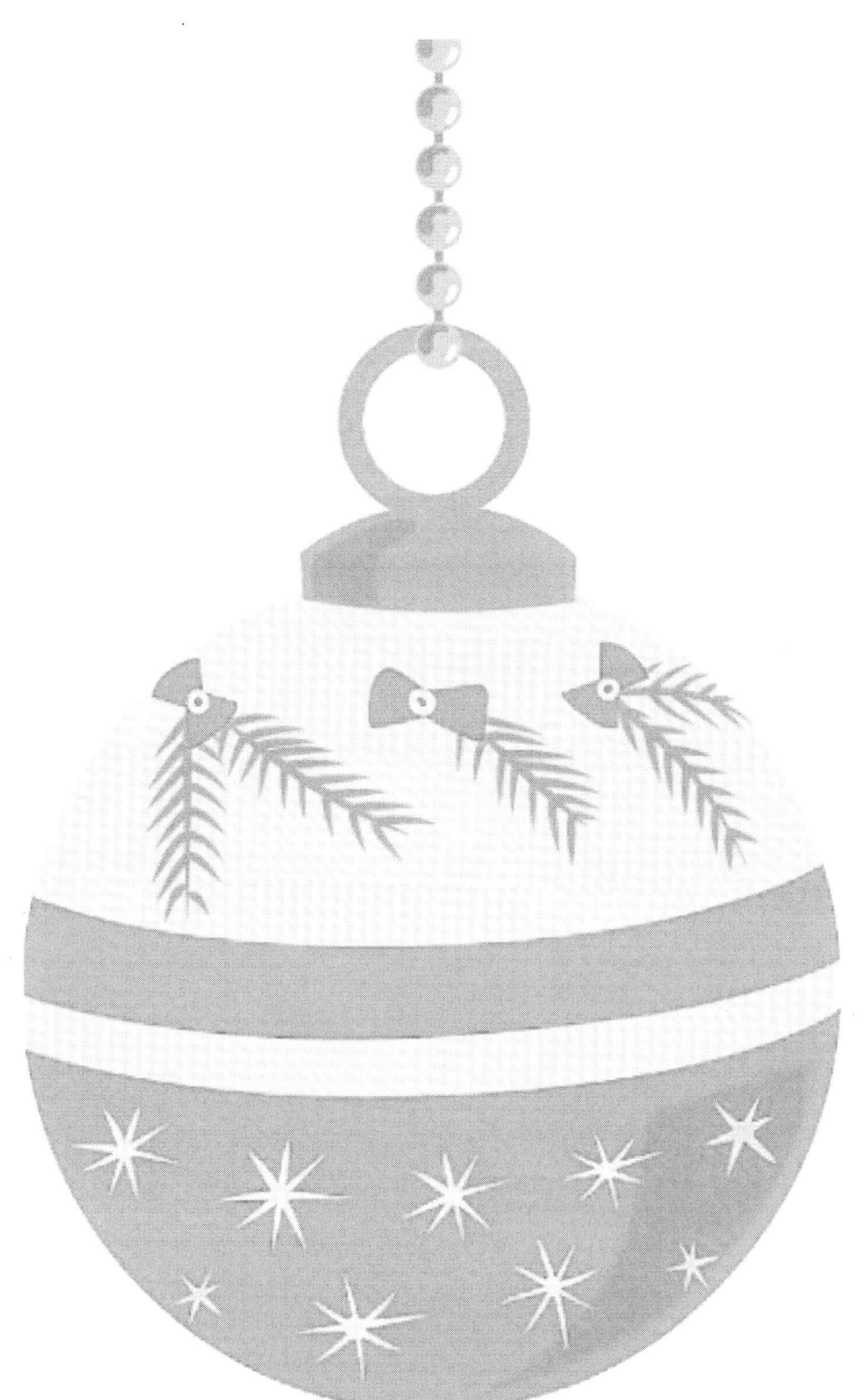

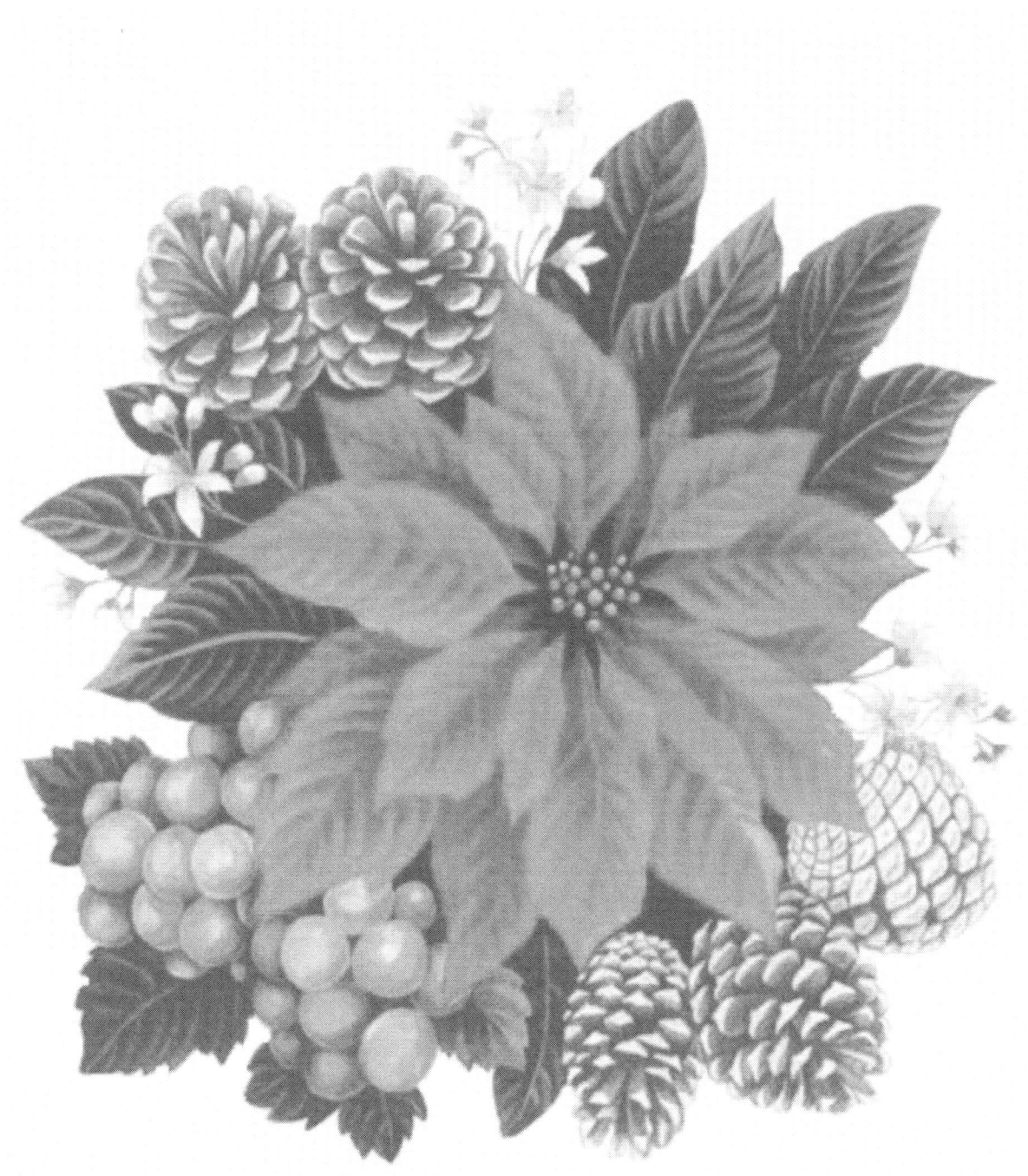

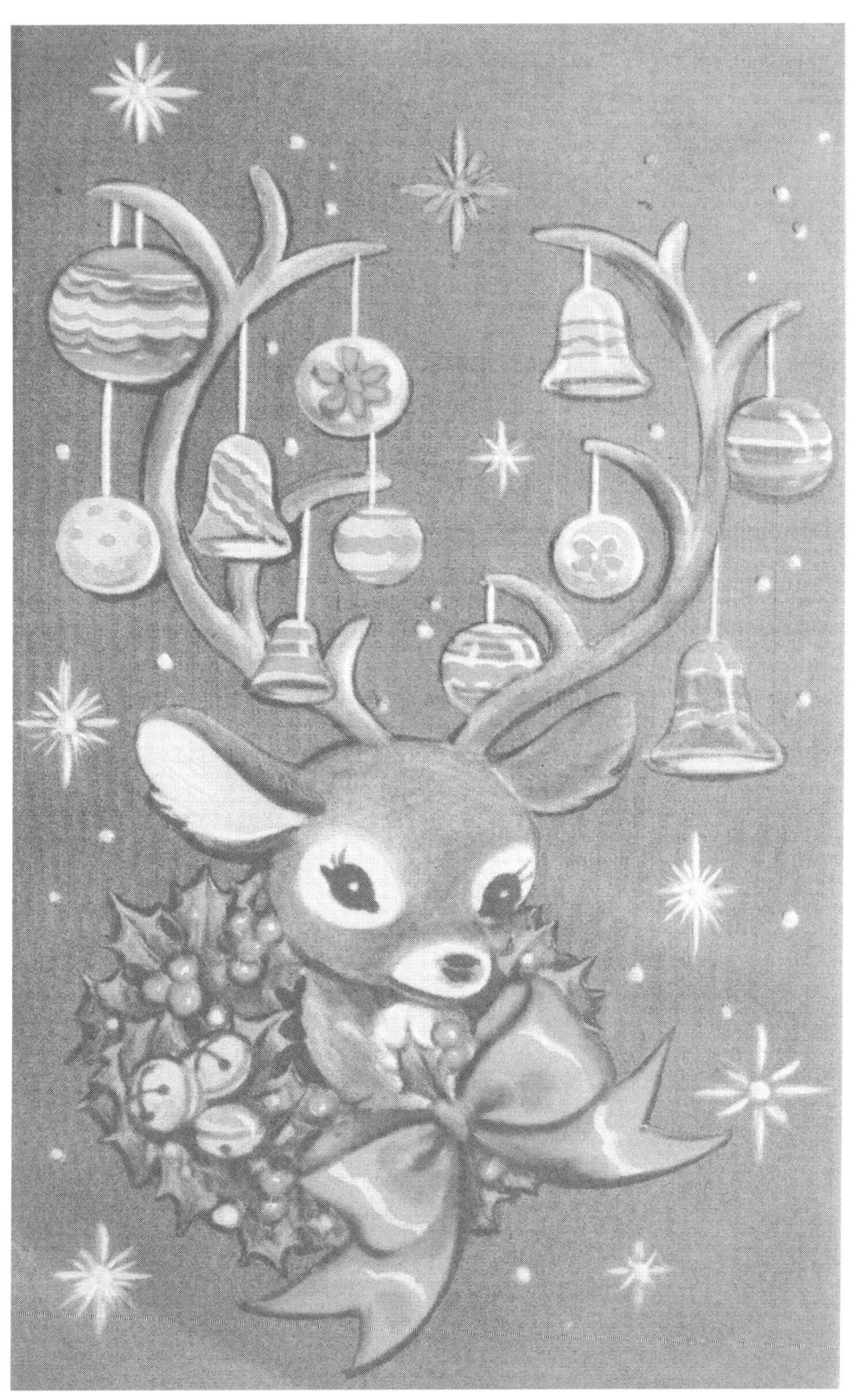

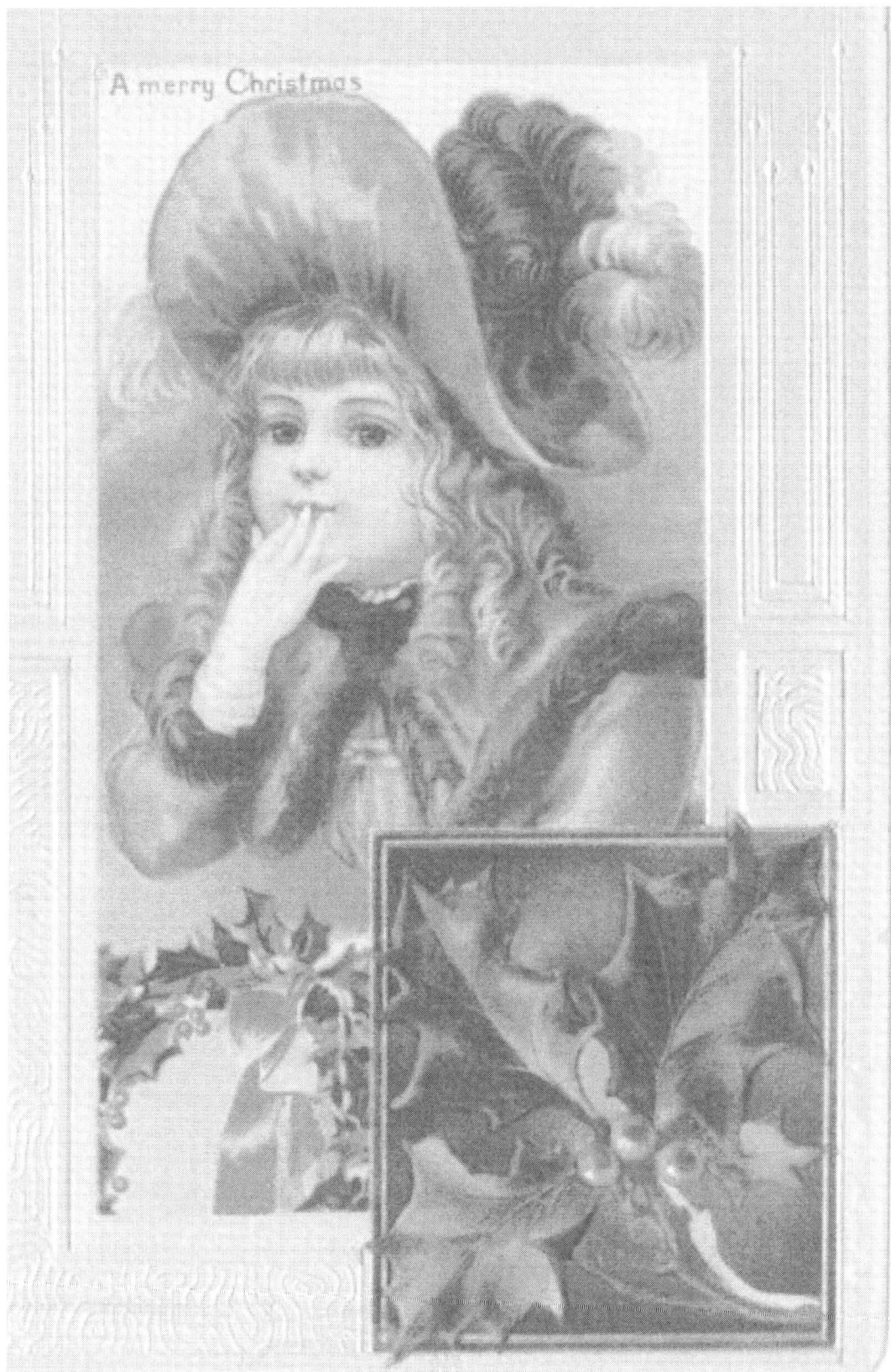

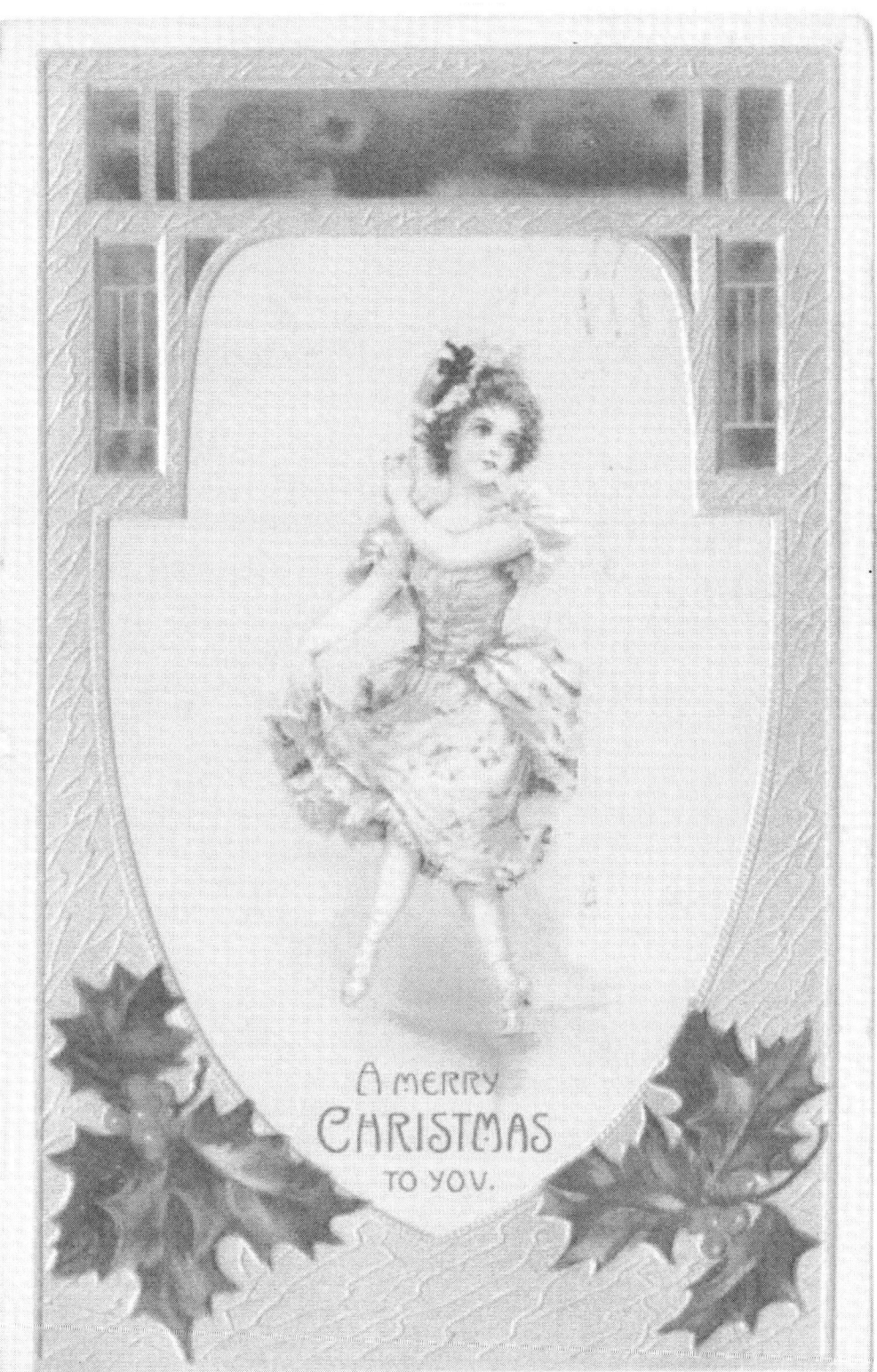

A MERRY
CHRISTMAS
TO YOU.

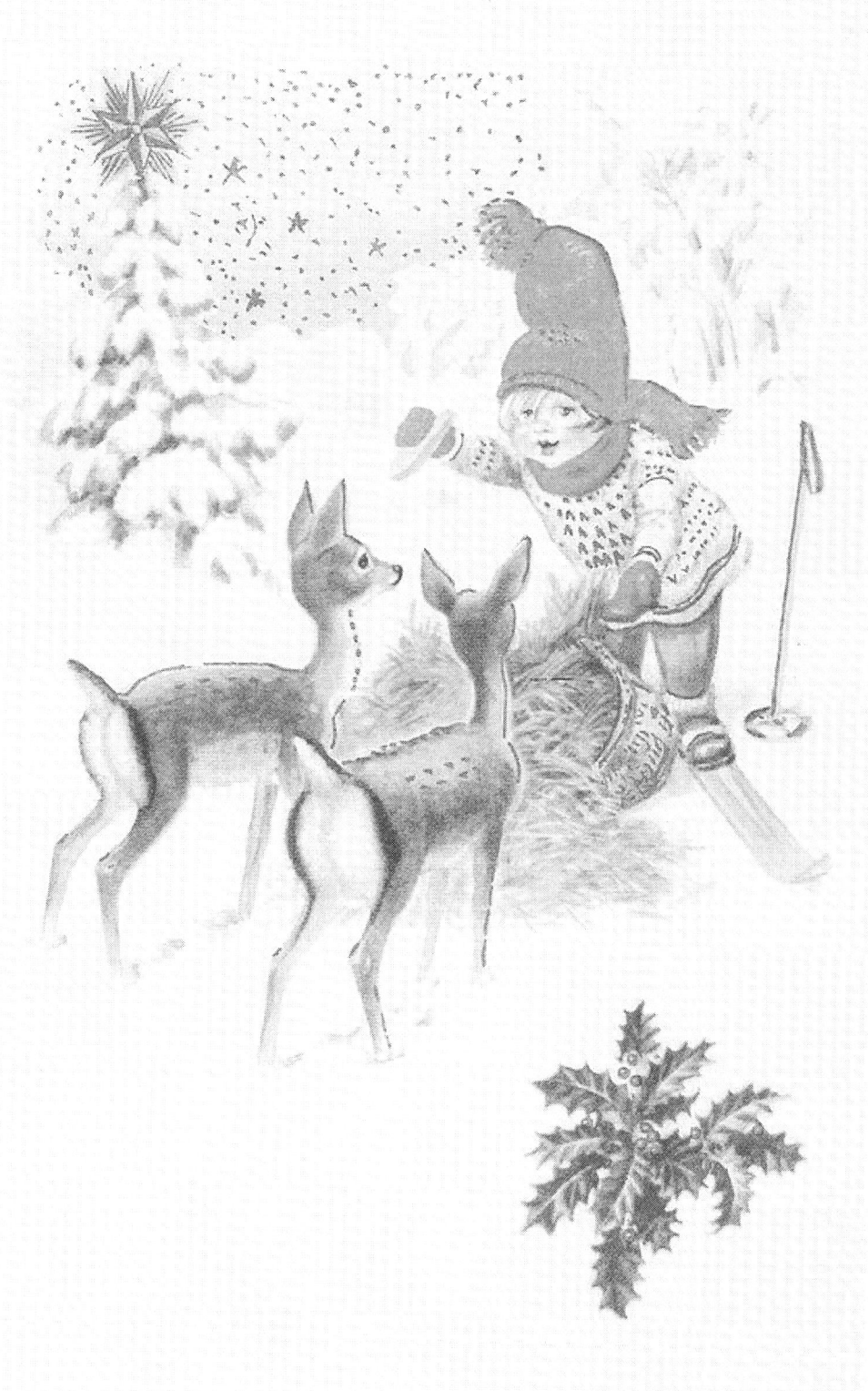

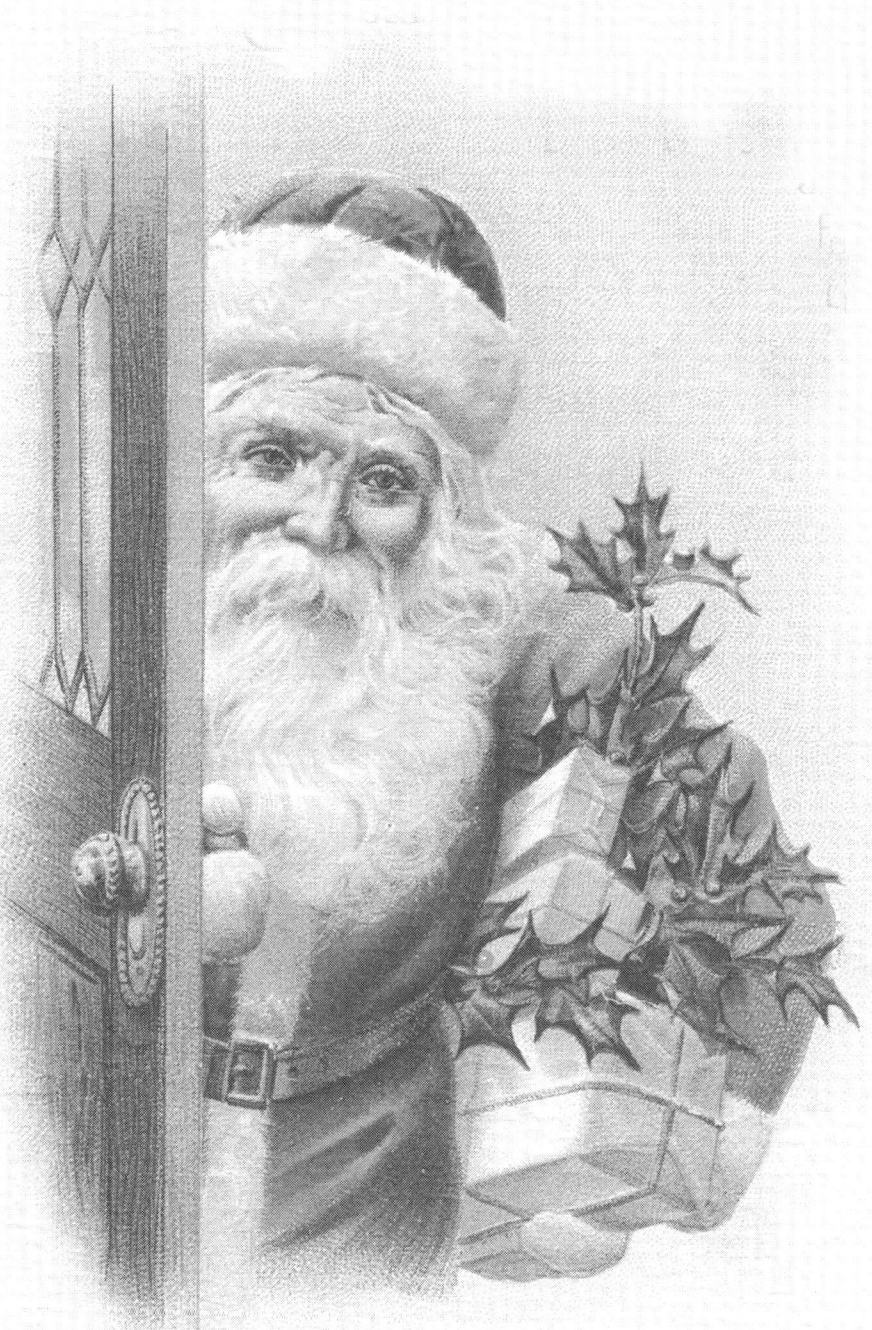

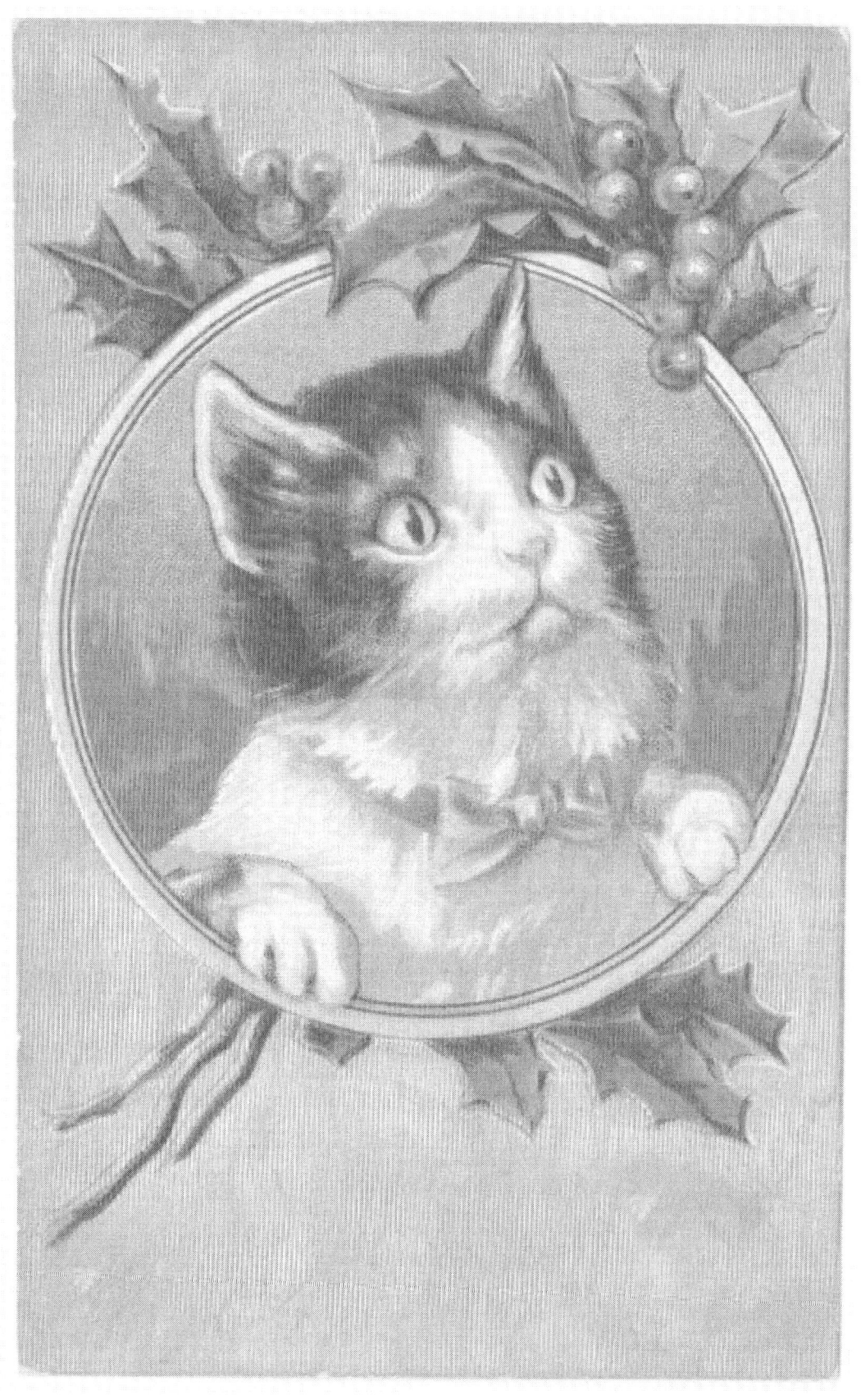

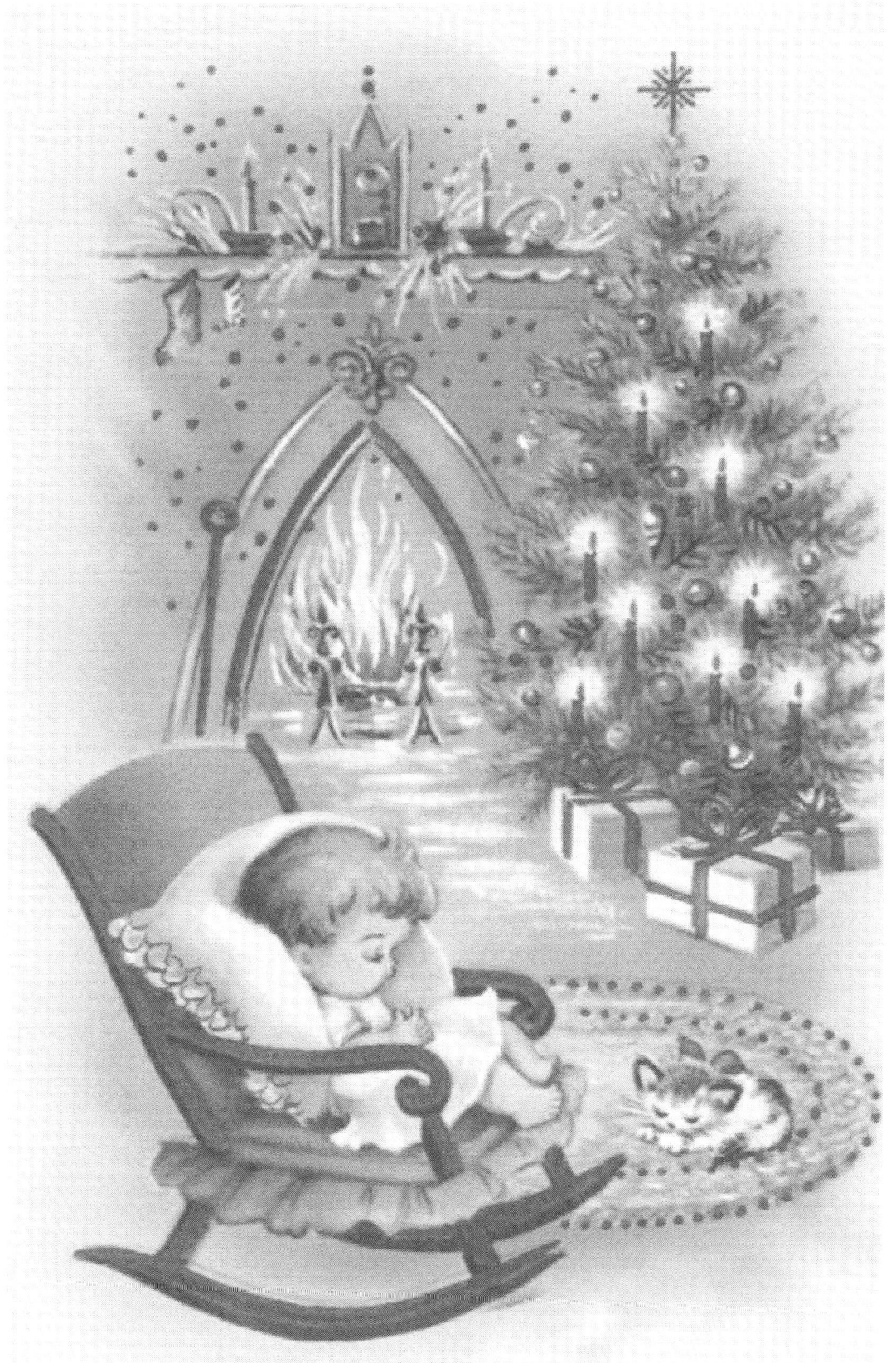

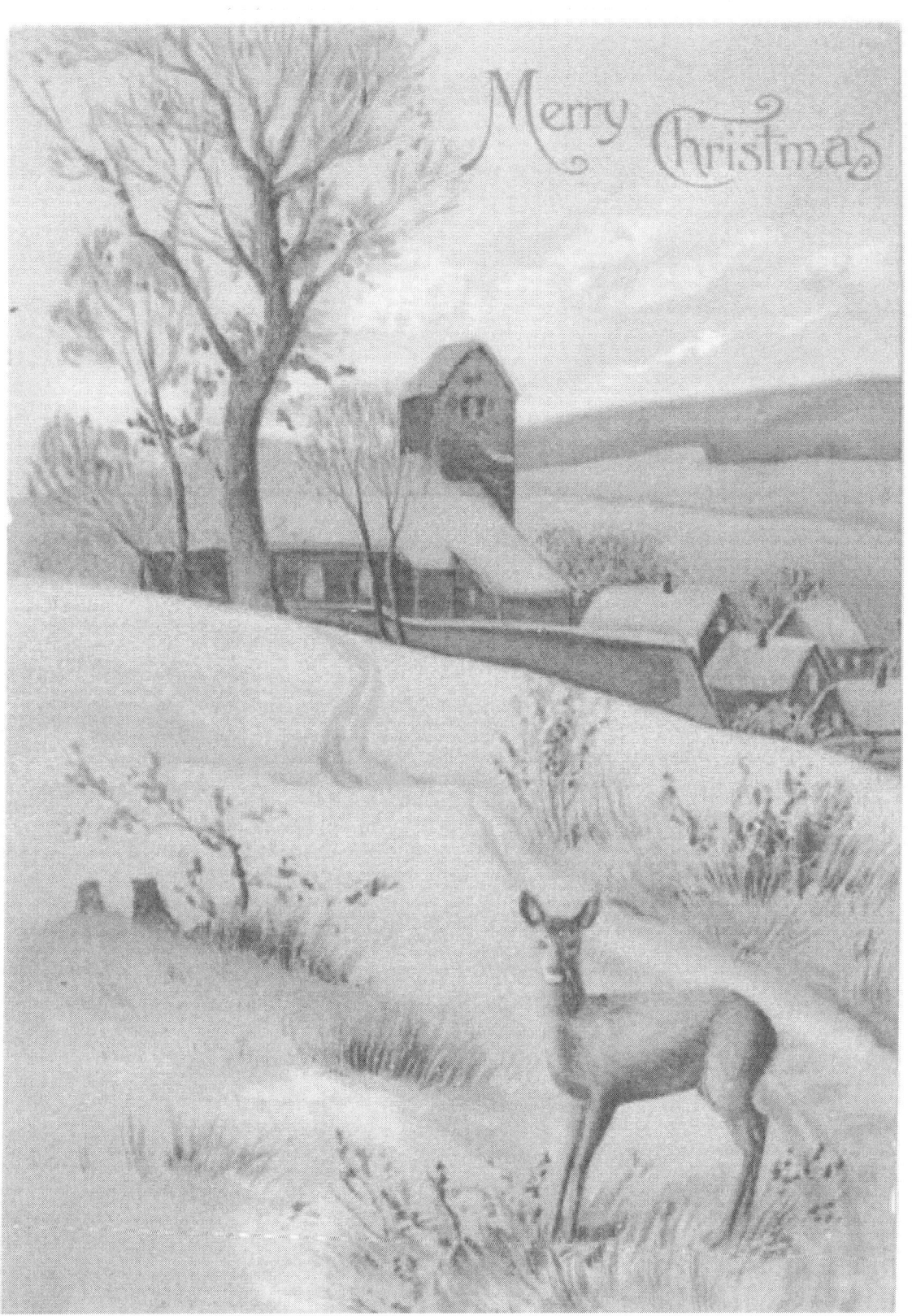

Book I in the Old Fashioned Christmas series. (Modern Pictures with a vintage feel) Available on Amazon.

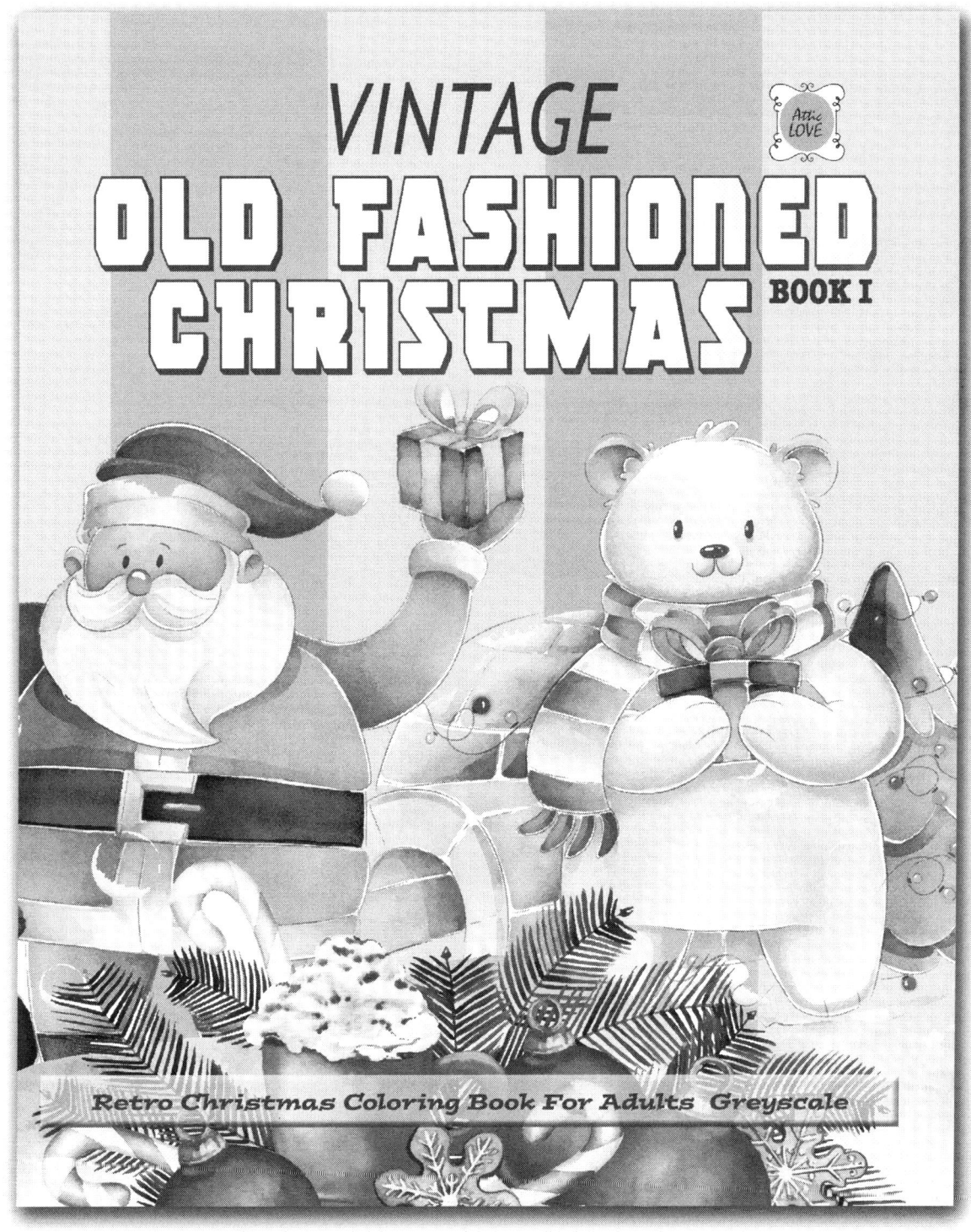

Book I in the Old Fashioned Christmas series. (Modern Pictures with a vintage feel) Available on Amazon.

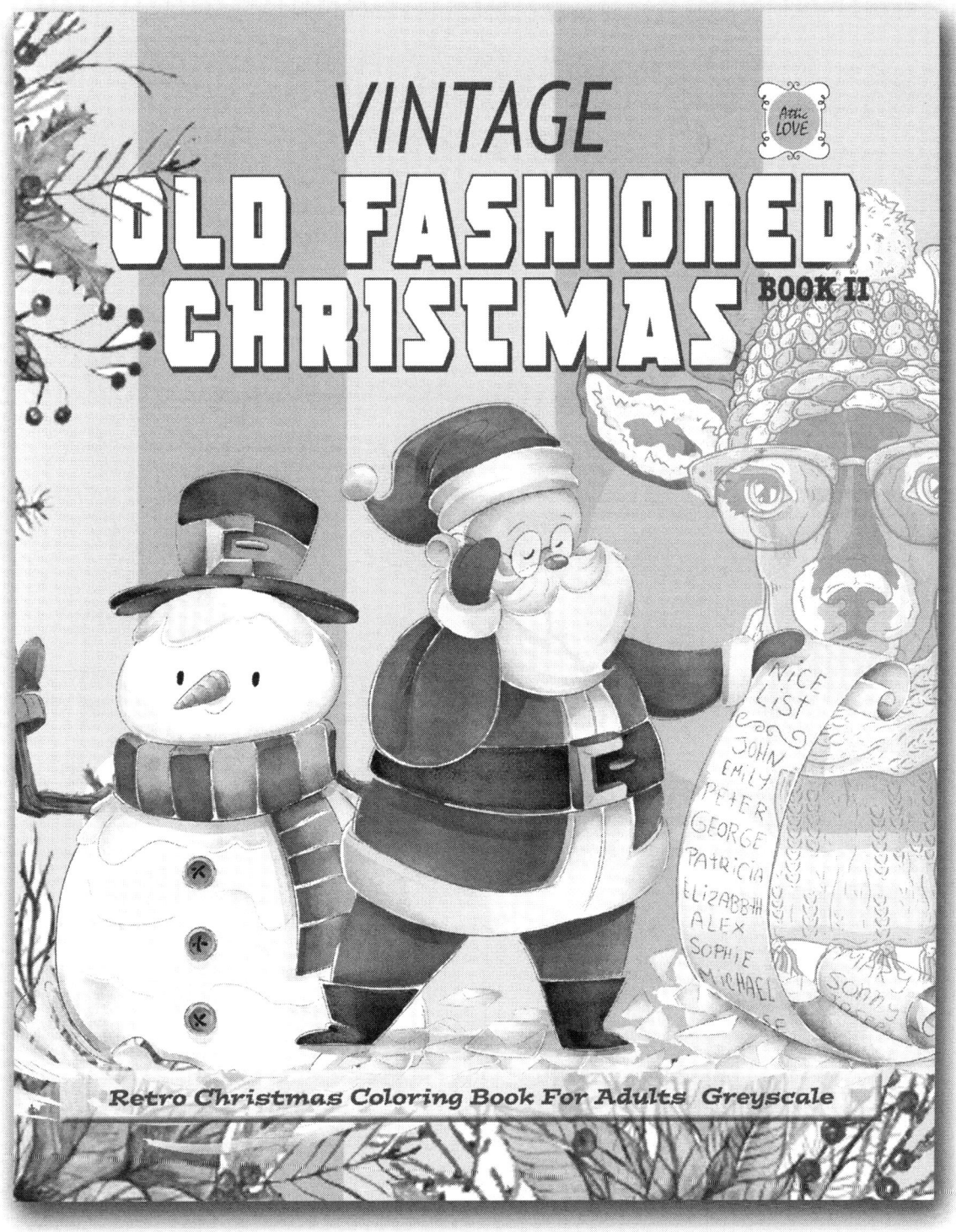

Attic
LOVE

• Tag your coloring pictures with #AtticLove on Facebook, Pinterest and Instagram for a change to have your images featured.

Manufactured by Amazon.ca
Bolton, ON

13752069R00039